WHAT IF THE
STOPPED SPIN...

Roopa Pai vaguely remembers graduating in computer engineering, but hasn't been able to prove it ever since aliens made off with her degree certificate. When she isn't writing books for children—she is the author of the fantasy-adventure series Taranauts—she is doing a bunch of other fun things, like leading history and heritage walks for other people's children or bawling out her own. She lives and works in Bangalore, her most favourite city in the world.

Kavita Singh Kale has been illustrating and writing for children's books, music videos and short films for over a decade now. She has a BFA in painting from New Delhi and a PG degree in Animation from the National Institute of Design, Ahmedabad.

Other books in the series

How Did the Harappans Say Hello?
And 16 Other Mysteries of History

Do Tigers Drink Blood?
And 13 Other Mysteries of Nature

WHAT IF THE EARTH STOPPED SPINNING?

AND 24 OTHER MYSTERIES OF SCIENCE

Roopa Pai

Illustrated by
Kavita Singh Kale

RED TURTLE
RUPA

For Rohan,
who believes the real stuff is far more magical
than the most mastastic fantasy

CONTENTS

10 Mind-Numbing Mysteries
That Aren't Really Mysterious At All

SECTION I
10 NIGHTMARISH SCENARIOS THAT YOU SHOULDN'T LOSE SLEEP OVER

WHAT IF THE SUN SUDDENLY DISAPPEARED?

Oooh. That would be a catastrophe of quite ASTRONOMICAL proportions, considering that most life on earth–including us human beings–depends on the sun for light, warmth, energy, oxygen and food. What's that you say? You're packing your bags and getting on to the next spaceship to Mars? Erm, waste of time. Mars is also a part of the solar system and depends on the same sun. You'll head for another star system then, and take your chances with finding a planet that can sustain human life? Good luck with that. You only have like a dodecaquadrisesquillion* possible star systems to check out.

But while you're packing, just to pass the time, let's try and imagine what would ACTUALLY happen to the earth if the sun got into a very bad mood and decided to disappear.

WHAT WOULD HAPPEN TO THE EARTH IF THE SUN DISAPPEARED: A BLOW-BY-BLOW ACCOUNT

1. Well, for starters, we wouldn't even know about it for a bit. Light from the sun takes about 8 minutes and 20 seconds to reach the earth, so we would only realize that the sun had

---

*A word we just made up to denote a Very Large Number because we're too lazy to find out what the actual number is. Look it up yourself on the Internet.

gone 8 minutes and 20 seconds AFTER the sun had actually disappeared.

2. Around the same time that we realized that the sun had gone, something equally terrible would also happen. The earth would shoot out of its orbit around the sun and fly off into space at 30 km per second. (Are you thinking, 'Huh? Why would THAT happen?' The explanation in a box later in this section.)

3. With no sunlight, there would be no moonlight as well, since moonlight is just the sun's light reflecting off the surface of the moon.

4. It would be night all over the world, ALL the time. Some little light would still come to us from faraway stars, so we would still be able to see a little. Plus, we would still have plenty of artificial light: electricity would continue to be generated since it is entirely man-made (cheers to us!) and doesn't depend on the sun.

5. Photosynthesis, the process by which plants prepare food for themselves and for us *in the presence of sunlight*, would completely stop. Without sunlight, plants would also not be able to take in carbon-dioxide or give out precious oxygen. But the good news is that there is enough oxygen in the atmosphere for all oxygen-breathing earth creatures to live for thousands of years, even without a single plant or tree giving out oxygen.

6. Phew! So *we* can breathe easy, but not the poor plants. Most of them would be dead in a few weeks, not just because of the lack of sunlight, but because they would, like most of the earth's creatures, freeze to death.

7. Because, within a week of the sun's disappearance, the average temperature of the earth would drop to below freezing. Sure, we would be able to keep warm and survive for a while—many places on earth are used to below freezing temperatures in winter—but by the time a year has passed, the average temperature would have dropped to below -73 C! Brrrr!

8. One way to stay warm and escape an icy death would be to move to places where geothermal energy—heat generated deep inside the earth—is high, like Iceland. But it is unlikely that the Icelanders will be allowing too many other humans to share their heat, so unless you are very famous or very rich or very, very clever, you might as well resign yourself to being dead within a year of the sun's disappearance.

9. Around the same time, the world's oceans will freeze over. But the thick layer of ice floating on the surface will prevent heat from leaving the deepest, darkest parts of the ocean, which are warmed by the earth's core. Since the creatures that live there have never experienced the sun's light and warmth, they won't mind one bit—or even notice!—that the sun has gone, and will keep swimming around happily for thousands of years to come.

10. The lucky humans who manage to find a home in a geothermal area may be able to survive for several years, but it will become harder and harder as the earth gets colder. But given human ingenuity and intelligence, chances are that they will use those years to come up with some fabulous new technology that will help the species to not just survive, but thrive, on the sunless earth.

WHY YOU SHOULD NOT LOSE SLEEP OVER THE 'DISAPPEARING SUN' NIGHTMARE

The sun is only a middle-aged star now, just 4.5 billion years old, the same age as the earth. It will easily take another 5 billion years, for the sun to die. Well before that, though, it will use up all the 'fuel' in its centre and begin to get bigger and bigger and hotter and hotter.

In about 1.2 billion years from now, the sun will be big enough and hot enough to melt all the earth's ice caps and boil away its oceans. Then it will get so big (20 times bigger than it is today, according to estimates) that it will swallow up Mercury, Venus and possibly the earth as well! Only then will it completely die out.

But see, the good part about a bigger, hotter sun is that the outer planets and moons of the solar system will become good places to live in. And in a billion years from now, do you seriously believe we wouldn't have established colonies on *some* of them at least? So cross that one off your worry list.

WHY WOULD THE EARTH FLY OFF INTO SPACE IF THE SUN DISAPPEARED?

SHORT ANSWER: BECAUSE IF THE SUN DISAPPEARED, ITS GREAT MASS WOULD DISAPPEAR TOO, AND WITH IT, ITS GRAVITATIONAL PULL ON THE EARTH. WITHOUT THE SUN'S GRAVITATIONAL FORCE PULLING ON IT, THE EARTH WOULD FLY OFF INTO SPACE, JUST LIKE THE HAMMER FLIES OFF WHEN A HAMMER-THROWER LETS GO OF THE WIRE IN A SPORTING COMPETITION.

LONG ANSWER: THE MASS OF AN OBJECT IS THE AMOUNT OF MATTER IN IT. THE BIGGER OR DENSER AN OBJECT, THE GREATER IS ITS MASS. MASS IS MEASURED IN KILOGRAMS, JUST LIKE WEIGHT IS, BUT THE TWO AREN'T THE SAME. THE WEIGHT OF AN OBJECT CHANGES DEPENDING ON THE AMOUNT OF GRAVITATIONAL FORCE THE OBJECT IS FEELING. FOR INSTANCE, YOUR WEIGHT ON THE EARTH IS MORE THAN YOUR WEIGHT ON THE MOON, BECAUSE THE EARTH PULLS ON YOU WITH MORE GRAVITATIONAL FORCE THAN THE MOON DOES. BUT THE MASS OF AN OBJECT—THE AMOUNT OF MATTER IN IT—REMAINS THE SAME WHETHER THE OBJECT FEELS A LARGE GRAVITATIONAL PULL OR NONE AT ALL.

WHY DOES THE EARTH PULL ON YOU WITH MORE GRAVITATIONAL FORCE THAN THE MOON? BECAUSE THE EARTH HAS A MUCH GREATER MASS THAN THE MOON. (USUALLY, BIGGER OBJECTS HAVE MORE MASS). IN FACT, EVERY OBJECT IN THE UNIVERSE THAT HAS MASS PULLS ON EVERY OTHER

OBJECT IN THE UNIVERSE WITH SOME AMOUNT OF GRAVITATIONAL FORCE. OBJECTS WITH GREATER MASS PULL WITH GREATER FORCE, AND OBJECTS WITH SMALLER MASSES PULL WITH A SMALLER FORCE.

THE REASON THAT THE EARTH REVOLVES AROUND THE SUN INSTEAD OF THE OTHER WAY ROUND IS THAT THE SUN'S MASS (AND, AS A RESULT, ITS GRAVITATIONAL FORCE) IS SO MUCH GREATER THAN THE EARTH'S.

BUT HOW COME THE EARTH DOESN'T JUST FALL INTO THE SUN THEN, YOU ASK? BECAUSE THE EARTH'S MASS—AND THEREFORE *ITS* GRAVITATIONAL FORCE—IS LARGE ENOUGH TO RESIST BEING ENTIRELY PULLED IN.

AND THAT'S WHY, IF THE SUN, AND ITS GINORMOUS MASS, DISAPPEARED, THE EARTH WOULD FLY OFF INTO SPACE, BECAUSE THERE WOULD BE NO FORCE KEEPING IT IN ORBIT ANY LONGER. CHANCES ARE THAT, SOONER OR LATER, SOME OTHER CELESTIAL OBJECT BIGGER

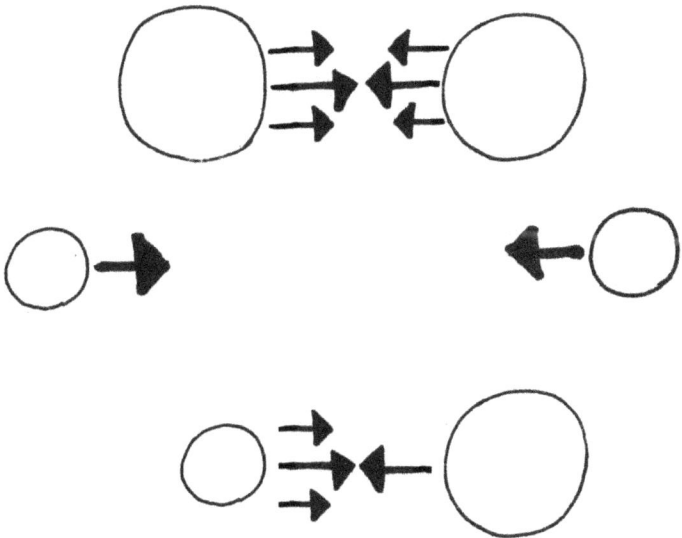

The bigger you are, the more 'attractive' you get!

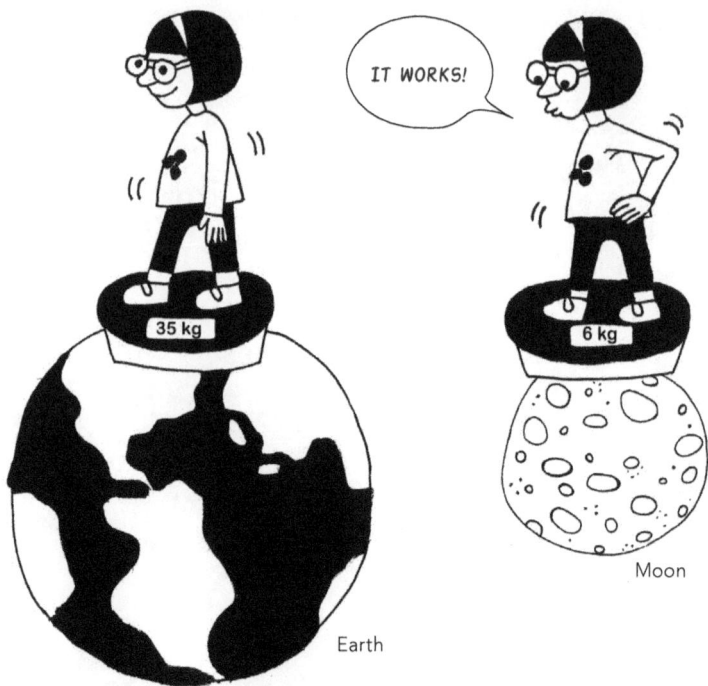

Move to the moon! Instant weight-loss 100% guaranteed!

THAN THE EARTH WOULD PULL IT INTO ITS ORBIT. AND IF THE OBJECT WAS A STAR AND THE DISTANCE WAS RIGHT, A BRAND NEW—AND TOTALLY EXCITING—CHAPTER COULD BEGIN IN THE OLD, OLD STORY OF THE EARTH.

WHAT IF THE MOON FELL OUT OF ITS ORBIT AND CRASHED INTO THE EARTH?

Ouch. Remember the dinosaurs? Remember one of the popular theories going around about why they suddenly became extinct? Yeah, the one about a giant asteroid hitting the earth, causing earthquakes and tsunamis and blasting chunks of rock high into the atmosphere from where they fell right back to earth, creating a firestorm and killing off 80 per cent of all life on earth at one go. In fact, you can still see the 180-km-wide crater left by that impact: it's in Mexico, and it is called the Chicxulub crater.

Well, just to put things in perspective, that asteroid or comet or whatever-it-was that crashed into the earth 65 million years ago was a mere 9 km long. The moon is a solid rock-and-metal sphere which is—hold your breath—3,476 km in diameter! So if the moon crashed into the earth, there is no doubt that all—and that means ALL—life on earth would be destroyed. But what EXACTLY would happen? Let's find out.

WHAT WOULD HAPPEN IF THE MOON COLLIDED WITH THE EARTH? A BLOW-BY-BLOW ACCOUNT

1. Well, first of all, if the moon had to collide with the earth, it would have to fall out of its orbit. (Why doesn't the moon fall out of its orbit anyway? What keeps it there, millennium after

9

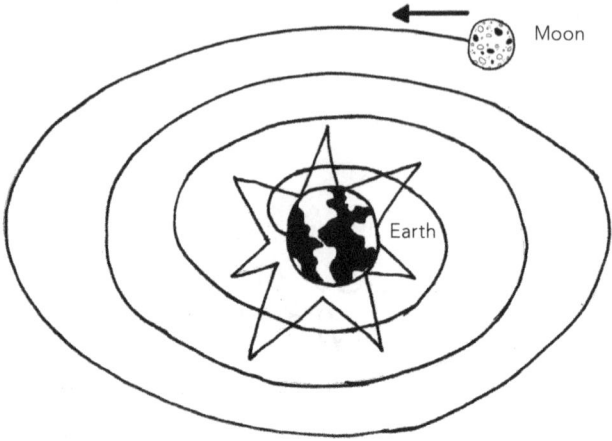

Death spiral of the moon

millennium, going round and round the earth and round and round the sun along the same path? Find out in the box on page 13.)

2. One of the ways in which the moon could fall out of its orbit is by losing speed. However, if the moon's speed of revolution fell, it would not instantly plummet to earth like a stone. Instead, it would begin to fall towards the earth in an ever-tightening spiral, a process that could take several days or months. In other words, there will be enough time for us to shriek, tear our hair, and panic madly.

3. Now, well before the moon *actually* collided with us, drastic stuff would begin to happen on earth just from the moon getting closer. You see, we humans have arrived on the earth at a very good time, AFTER our planet and our moon and our yellow star have figured out the ideal distances and forces between themselves for all three of them to remain stable and for earth to sustain life. Even a minor change in that delicate balance would upset everything, and the moon falling out of its orbit is not exactly what we would call a *minor* change.

4. What kind of stuff would happen? To understand that, we must first understand how the moon actually affects us, apart from making us go 'ooh' and 'aah' and write poems about its beauty. You see, even though the moon is some 384,000 km away from us, its gravitational pull on the earth is pretty strong.

5. When the moon passes over the earth's oceans each day, its gravitational pull 'pulls' up the water, causing tides. It is the moon's gravitational pull that keeps the earth tilted at an angle of exactly 23.4 degrees, and it is because of that tilt that we have seasons. When the northern half of the earth is tilted towards the sun (April to September) that half complains about the heat and buys tons of ice cream and goes to the beach and has summer vacations while the southern half shivers, and when the southern half is tilted towards the sun (October to March), that part plans picnics and pulls out the

summer clothes and has Christmas on the beach while the northern half shovels snow off its driveways and huddles in its razais and drinks gallons of masala chai. The same pull also keeps the earth rotating at the speed that it does (24 hours per rotation).

6. So, if the moon started coming closer to us, exerting a greater gravitational pull than before (because gravitational pull increases as distance between two objects decreases), we could expect some really spectacular stunts from Mother Nature—5-km-high tsunami waves, extinct volcanoes coming to life as the moon pulled on the magma deep inside the earth, and a real earth 'quake' as our poor planet began to wobble madly about its axis.

7. And if the moon came even closer, countries, land masses, even entire continents, would be ripped apart. Because the earth would be pulling really hard on the moon as well, the moon would begin to approach faster and faster. As it entered the earth's atmosphere, its outer layers would begin to burn because of the friction, turning the moon into a gigantic fireball. The good thing about all this is that if the tsunamis and the earthquakes and the volcanoes hadn't killed you yet, pure naked fear as you watch the fireball approach will definitely finish you off BEFORE the disastrous impact.

8. On impact, the pressure on the earth's core would be so high that it would turn everything on the earth's surface—rocks, mountains, forests—into boiling liquid. As the moon and the earth merged, the earth would develop an unsightly lump—a moon tumour—where the moon hit. Since the resulting celestial body—the Earthoon?—would not be a sphere anymore, its rotation would go completely awry.

9. Gigantic chunks of the earth and moon would fly off into space, creating new moons and asteroids and UFOs. In fact, our moon is believed to have been created by just this kind of space accident billions of years ago.

WHY YOU SHOULD NOT LOSE SLEEP OVER THE 'FALLING MOON' NIGHTMARE

Because the basic premise—that the moon will slow down for some inexplicable reason and begin to fall towards earth—is very unlikely. What is in fact happening is that the moon is going *further away* from the earth, its orbit shifting outwards by about 3.7 cm a year. But that doesn't mean you should start worrying about what will happen if the moon floats away, because THAT isn't going to happen for many billions of years.

WHY DOES THE MOON NOT FALL TOWARDS THE EARTH?

SHORT ANSWER: BECAUSE THERE ARE TWO VERY STRONG, PERFECTLY-BALANCED FORCES WORKING TOGETHER TO KEEP IT WHERE IT IS: IN CONTINUOUS ORBIT AROUND THE EARTH. UNLESS THE MOON SLOWED DOWN FOR SOME REASON, OR GOT KNOCKED OUT OF ITS ORBIT BY ANOTHER, BIGGER CELESTIAL BODY, IT WILL STAY RIGHT WHERE IT IS.

LONG ANSWER: HERE'S THE THING. THE MOON AND THE EARTH ARE CONSTANTLY PULLING AT EACH OTHER WITH THEIR RESPECTIVE GRAVITATIONAL FORCES. BECAUSE THE EARTH IS SO MUCH BIGGER THAN THE MOON, ITS GRAVITATIONAL FORCE IS MUCH GREATER THAN THE MOON'S (SEE BOX ON PAGE 6 FOR MORE INFO ON THIS). IN FACT, IF THE MOON WAS STATIONARY, IT WOULD HAVE FALLEN INTO EARTH LONG AGO BECAUSE OF THE EARTH'S STONGER GRAVITATIONAL PULL.

BUT THE MOON IS NOT STATIONARY. IT IS MOVING AT A HIGH SPEED OF 3,600 KM PER HOUR THROUGH SPACE. IF IT WASN'T FOR THE EARTH'S GRAVITY, THE MOON WOULD HAVE ZIPPED OFF INTO OUTER SPACE IN A STRAIGHT LINE.

AT EVERY INSTANT AS IT GOES AROUND THE EARTH, THE MOON IS TRYING TO GET AWAY AND THE EARTH IS TRYING TO PULL IT IN. AT EVERY INSTANT, THE MOON BEGINS TO FALL TOWARDS THE

EARTH BUT DOESN'T BECAUSE THE OTHER FORCE—THE FORCE OF ITS MOVEMENT IN A STRAIGHT LINE—PUSHES IT AWAY. IN FACT, THE VERY REASON THAT THE MOON GOES AROUND THE EARTH IS THAT THESE TWO FORCES—THE 'PULLING IN' FORCE AND THE 'PUSHING OUT' FORCE—ARE PERFECTLY BALANCED.

THIS IS JUST LIKE WHAT HAPPENS WHEN YOU TIE A BALL TO THE END OF A STRING AND SWING IT AROUND YOUR HEAD. CUT THE STRING (REMOVE THE EARTH'S GRAVITATIONAL PULL) AND THE BALL (MOON) WILL FLY OFF. STOP SWINGING THE BALL AROUND (MAKE THE MOON STATIONARY) AND IT WILL IMMEDIATELY DROP TOWARDS YOU (THE EARTH). TRY IT YOURSELF!

WHAT IF ALL THE WORLD'S NUCLEAR BOMBS WENT OFF TOGETHER?

Help! Considering that just two small atom bombs dropped on the Japanese cities Hiroshima and Nagasaki in 1945 killed some 250,000 people and flattened large parts of both cities, this scenario is worse than any nightmare you could possibly have when you are asleep!

And what's more: Little Boy, the bomb dropped on Hiroshima (yes, the bomb actually had a name!) had a mere 15 kilotons of power (1 kiloton = the explosive power of 1,000 tons of TNT); in 1961, just sixteen years later, Russia (or the Soviet Union, as it was then called) tested the Tsar Bomba, a nuclear bomb which had 57,000 kilotons of power and could damage an area of close to 9,500 sq km! To date, the Tsar Bomba remains the most destructive weapon built by humans to destroy themselves and their planet.

WHAT ACTUALLY HAPPENS WHEN A NUCLEAR BOMB GOES OFF: A BLOW-BY-BLOW ACCOUNT

1. For the purpose of this account, let's assume the bomb was dropped over a city, where it would cause maximum damage to life and property.
2. Now, nuclear bombs cause maximum damage when they

explode in the air above the target; they would be less destructive if they hit the ground. How badly affected you are depends on how far you are from the centre of the bomb blast, which is called the 'hypocentre' or, more popularly, 'ground zero'. The closer you are to ground zero, the less your chances of survival.

3.   There are many reasons for severe bodily damage from a nuclear explosion. One of the biggest, and most immediate, is the wave of intense heat (300 million degrees Celsius) from the explosion. Human beings, animals, buildings, trees, rocks–everything in the vicinity of the hypocentre wouldn't just be burned, but instantly VAPORIZED. If you were a little further away, you would only get charred to death.

4.   Another cause of death and destruction is the high pressure wave resulting from the rapid expansion of the overheated air around the blast. This pressure wave would slam into buildings and people, ripping them apart.

5.   If the heat and the pressure don't get you, chances are you will be levelled by a flying piece of building debris, or by severe exposure to nuclear radiation. (What exactly is nuclear radiation? And how does it kill humans? See on page 18 to find out.)

6.   If you escape that too, don't start partying. There is always nuclear fallout to worry about. Fallout, or Black Rain, is the name for the tiny particles of radioactive material from the bomb that shoot miles up into the sky at the explosion and then slowly begin to float back down to earth after the first blast of heat and pressure have passed. These particles can cause severe damage, so stay indoors for at least five weeks to be perfectly safe. But by then, radioactive dust could have got into the water and the food, so you're not going to be perfectly safe after all.

7.   Now, all that heat generated from the blast would obviously result in quite a few massive fires for a radius of tens of kilometres around the blast site. If enough bombs are

dropped on cities, and enough fires happen, the dense sooty smoke rising from them would be whipped away by the wind high into the upper layers of the atmosphere, where the soot particles would remain for years and years, blocking the sun's light and heat. Temperatures on earth would drop drastically, photosynthesis would slow down, affecting the food chain, and a terrible 'nuclear winter' lasting several months would follow. Of course, this has never happened, and it is only what scientists believe will happen after a full-blown nuclear war, but, as we all know, scientists tend to be smart people.

8. Radiation and radioactive fallout would disappear eventually, but their effects would linger on in people exposed even to small amounts of it, and in their unborn children. Many more people in the area would develop cancer, many babies would be born deformed, and all kinds of other diseases and disabilities would result from eating grains and vegetables grown in soil contaminated with radiation.

9. Yeah, so, nuclear war: NOT a good idea for anyone. And that is probably the One Big Reason why no one is going to start one in a hurry.

WHY YOU SHOULD NOT LOSE SLEEP OVER THE MEGA NUCLEAR HOLOCAUST NIGHTMARE

1. Like we said before, a nuclear war would be SO bad for humanity that no one is likely to start one any time soon. Only nine countries in the world have nuclear warheads (a nuclear warhead is the explosive head of a missile or torpedo carrying an atom bomb). Two of them are India and Pakistan, the others are USA, Russia, UK, France, China, North Korea, and possibly Israel.

2. According to official figures, there are about 17,000 nuclear warheads in the world, of which 16,000 belong to either the USA or to Russia. Of these 17,000 warheads, only a little over 4,000 are 'active' or 'deployed' (which means 'in position and

ready to use'), (Oh, and just for your information, none of these active warheads are in India or Pakistan.) The rest have been dismantled and are lying in nuclear 'stockpiles' until the nuclear fuel in them can be 'recycled' for more useful things: like generating electricity.

3. The number of nuclear warheads is only going to reduce in the future. In the 1990s, USA and Russia ended what was called 'The Arms Race' by signing a document called START or the Strategic Arms Reduction Treaty, in which both countries agreed to reduce the number of nuclear weapons in their arsenals. Later, China, UK and France also promised not to build any more nuclear weapons. It is because of START that the number of active nuclear warheads in the world has come down from 68,000 (in 1985) to 4,000 (in 2013).

4. Officially, only one Tsar Bomba was ever built, and it was the one that was tested. There are no more left in the world. Even if there were a couple still lying about, they would not be able to destroy the earth; it would take more than 300 Tsar Bombas just to destroy India, and some 16,000 of them to destroy the whole world. The 4,000 warheads we still have are each much less powerful than the Tsar.

5. Even if there were 16,000 Tsar Bombas and they were ALL used, nothing would happen to the earth. She is a Very Big Ball of rock and iron and it would take more than 16,000 puny earthling bombs to destroy her. The puny earthlings themselves, however, would be completely destroyed.

WHAT IS NUCLEAR RADIATION? AND HOW DOES IT AFFECT HUMANS?

ALL MATTER IS MADE UP OF ATOMS. ATOMS ARE MADE UP OF SMALLER PARTICLES CALLED PROTONS, NEUTRONS AND ELECTRONS. PROTONS AND NEUTRONS COME TOGETHER TO FORM THE NUCLEUS—OR HEAVY CORE—OF THE ATOM, AND ELECTRONS REVOLVE AROUND THIS NUCLEUS. PROTONS HAVE A POSITIVE CHARGE, AND ELECTRONS HAVE A

Somewhere in the world, at this very moment, 4,000 nuclear warheads are waiting. All it takes is one lunatic to press the red button...

TO FORM NEW ATOMS AND RELEASE ENERGY IN THE PROCESS (THIS IS WHAT HAPPENS ON A MEGA SCALE INSIDE THE SUN). THE OTHER WAY TO DO THIS IS THROUGH 'FISSION', WHERE ATOMS ARE SPLIT, ONCE AGAIN RELEASING ENERGY (THIS HAPPENS IN NUCLEAR POWER REACTORS AND, YES, NUCLEAR BOMBS).

NOW, THE ATOM OF EVERY ELEMENT—IRON, ALUMINIUM, HYDROGEN, OXYGEN, CHLORINE—IS DIFFERENT; EACH HAS A DIFFERENT NUMBER AND COMBINATION OF PROTONS, NEUTRONS AND ELECTRONS.

MOST ELEMENTS HAVE STABLE ATOMS, THAT IS, THEIR PROTONS, NEUTRONS AND ELECTRONS ARE ONE TINY HAPPY FAMILY. IF YOU LEAVE AN ALUMINIUM ATOM ALONE FOR A MILLION YEARS AND THEN COME BACK AND LOOK AT IT, IT WILL STILL BE A CHEERFUL ALUMINIUM ATOM.

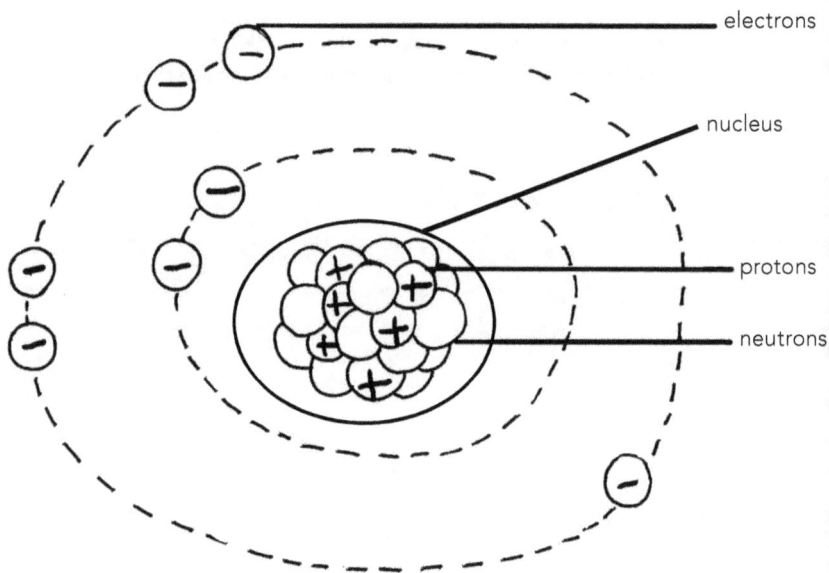

BUT A FEW ELEMENTS, LIKE URANIUM, HAVE ATOMS THAT ARE UNSTABLE. USUALLY, THE PROBLEM IS THAT THERE ARE TOO MANY NEUTRONS IN THE NUCLEUS. NOTHING IN NATURE LIKES TO BE UNSTABLE, SO THESE UNSTABLE ATOMS QUICKLY TRY TO GET STABLE, BY SPITTING OUT PROTONS, NEUTRONS OR ELECTRONS. THE STREAM OF REJECTED PARTICLES EXITING UNSTABLE ATOMS IS CALLED RADIATION. BECAUSE THESE PARTICLES COME FROM THE NUCLEUS, THE WHOLE THING GETS CALLED NUCLEAR RADIATION. ATOMS THAT CAUSE NUCLEAR RADIATION ARE CALLED RADIOACTIVE, AND IT IS THESE THAT ARE USED AS FUEL IN NUCLEAR BOMBS.

NOW, WHEN RADIOACTIVE ATOMS SPIT OUT WHATEVER THEY DO— ELECTRONS, PROTONS, NEUTRONS—THERE IS A LOT OF ENERGY RELEASED. THIS ENERGY CAUSES THESE TINY PARTICLES TO TRAVEL AT A VERY HIGH SPEED, CLOSE TO THE SPEED OF LIGHT (300,000 KM PER SECOND)! IF ANY OF YOUR BODY CELLS COME IN THE WAY OF THESE HIGH-SPEED, HIGH-ENERGY PARTICLES, THEY WILL BE RIPPED APART BEFORE THEY CAN CRY 'HELP'!

IF ONLY A FEW CELLS ARE AFFECTED, YOUR BODY WILL TRY TO REPAIR THEM. IF LOTS ARE, BE PREPARED FOR BURNS, BLOOD DISORDERS, CANCER, OR EVEN, IN SEVERE CASES OF RADIATION EXPOSURE, DEATH. SO STAY AWAY FROM NUCLEAR RADIATION, YOU HEAR?

Wham! Rogue neutron smashes into overweight uranium atom, splitting it.

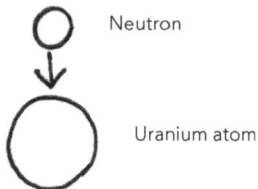

Neutron

Uranium atom

Whee! Three extra neutrons, suddenly free of the nucleus, take off.

Slam! Bam! Ka-pow! Each of these neutrons smash into a new uranium atom, splitting it, and freeing more neutrons.

Woohoo! MASSIVE amounts of energy are released.

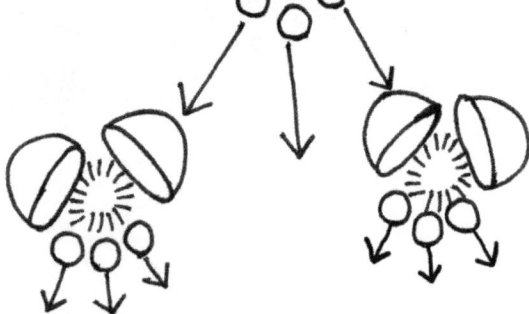

Fission—a ringside view:
How nuclear energy is released from a uranium atom

WHAT IF MY BUNCH OF BIRTHDAY BALLOONS CARRIED ME AWAY TO MICRONESIA?

Erm, that would be a pity, wouldn't it? Particularly if that happened before you had even had a teensy slice of your birthday cake!

But seriously, with people crossing the Atlantic and even the Pacific Ocean by hot air balloon (Richard Branson, the chairman of the £5 billion Virgin group of companies, holds the record for the fastest crossing of both), and with entire houses being carried away by balloons (this happens in the Pixar movie *Up*; if you haven't seen it, watch it *now*, and not just for the balloons-lifting-house scene either), it does seem like this particular nightmarish scenario is a real possibility.

But exactly how big would that bunch need to be? Let's try and come up with an actual number.

HOW MANY BALLOONS WOULD YOU ACTUALLY NEED TO LIFT YOU OFF THE GROUND?

First things first. You do know that the balloons would have to be filled with helium or hydrogen, don't you? They can't be filled with regular air. (As to why only helium and/or hydrogen balloons can lift you up, check the box on page 25).

Next we need to decide what size and shape of birthday

balloons we are using. Let's say, to make our calculations easier, that we are using round balloons. Let's say that these balloons, when fully inflated, become spheres which are roughly 30 cm (1 foot) in diameter.

How much helium would a balloon of this size hold? Using a complicated equation to calculate the volume of a sphere, we find that it holds about 14,000 cc (14 litres) of helium. Scientists have calculated that 1 litre of helium can lift roughly 1 gm of weight. That means our balloon, with 14 litres of helium in it, can lift about 14 gm of weight (in reality, it would be a little less than this, because the helium would also have to lift the weight of the balloon itself, but let's ignore that for now).

Now go and stand on a weighing scale and figure out how much you weigh. 30 kg? 40 kg? Let's say you weigh 35 kg. That's 35,000 gm. Which means you would need 35,000 litres of helium to lift your weight up. If each balloon can hold 14 litres, the number of balloons that can hold 35,000 litres is 35,000/14, so you will need—hold your breath—2,500 birthday balloons!

An adult weighing about 60 kg, would need no less than some 4,285 balloons to lift him or her off the ground!

AND WHAT IF I WANTED MY WHOLE HOUSE TO BE LIFTED AWAY, LIKE IN THE PIXAR MOVIE UP?

Well, it would depend on how big your house is, and how heavy it is, and what it is built of. In an interview he gave to Ballooning Magazine, director of *Up* Pete Docter revealed that technicians at Pixar estimated it would take around 23.5 *million*

balloons (of the same size as our balloons) to lift a 1,800-square-foot house like the one in the movie! But, Docter continued, when he and his team realized that actually putting in that many balloons in the animation would make them look like small coloured dots and not like balloons at all, they decided to put in fewer and forget about the physics of it.

In the scenes in the movie where the house is in flight, there are exactly 10,297 balloons. In the scene where the house actually lifts off, there are roughly double that number.

WHY YOU SHOULDN'T LOSE SLEEP OVER THE KIDNAPPED-BY-BALLOONS NIGHTMARE

Yes, 2,500 does not seem like a whole lot of balloons. But it is still unlikely that you will have so many helium balloons of that size at your birthday party. So don't worry, you aren't getting kidnapped by birthday balloons any time soon.

But the next time you see a bunch of 2,500 or more helium balloons in one place, maybe you should s-l-o-w-l-y turn around and walk right back the way you came. Just in case.

WHY DO HELIUM BALLOONS FLOAT ANYWAY?

HERE'S AN EXPERIMENT FOR YOU TO TRY: (BUT ONLY IF YOU CAN SWIM WELL AND YOUR MOM LETS YOU TRY THIS!) THE NEXT TIME YOU GO SWIMMING, TAKE AN EMPTY WATER BOTTLE WITH YOU. MAKE SURE THE LID IS SCREWED ON TIGHT, SO THAT NO WATER CAN GO IN. TIE A STRING AROUND THE NECK OF THE BOTTLE AND HOLD THE OTHER END IN YOUR HAND. SIT ON THE FLOOR OF THE POOL, STILL HOLDING THE END OF THE STRING IN YOUR HAND (AND HOLDING YOUR BREATH, TOO!) WHAT HAPPENS? THE BOTTLE FLOATS TO THE SURFACE OF THE POOL.

WHY DOES THIS HAPPEN?

SHORT ANSWER: BECAUSE OF AN UPWARDS FORCE CALLED BUOYANCY THAT EXISTS IN FLUIDS. BUOYANCY'S MAIN JOB IS TO OPPOSE THE DOWNWARD FORCE EXERTED BY THE WEIGHT OF AN OBJECT IN THE FLUID.

LONG ANSWER: WHEN YOU PUT AN OBJECT INTO A FLUID, THAT OBJECT NATURALLY TAKES UP SPACE IN THE FLUID. WHAT HAPPENS TO THE FLUID THAT ORIGINALLY OCCUPIED THAT SPACE? IT GETS MOVED ASIDE, OR DISPLACED. THIS IS WHY WATER SPILLS OVER THE SIDES OF A FULL BUCKET OF WATER WHEN YOU STEP INTO IT: YOUR LEGS DISPLACE THE WATER THAT USED TO BE WHERE YOUR LEGS NOW ARE. IN FACT, IF YOU COLLECTED THE WATER THAT SPILT OVER (DISPLACED WATER) AND WEIGHED IT, IT WOULD BE THE SAME WEIGHT AS THAT PART OF YOUR LEGS WHICH DID THE DISPLACING. WHICH, YOU WILL AGREE, IS A FAR MORE PAINLESS WAY TO FIGURE OUT HOW MUCH YOUR LEGS WEIGH THAN TO CUT THEM OFF AND WEIGH THEM ON A WEIGHING MACHINE!

THE PERSON WE HAVE TO THANK FOR THIS DISCOVERY IS ARCHIMEDES, THE GENIUS FROM ANCIENT GREECE. LET'S PAUSE A MINUTE HERE FOR HIS STORY. ONE COLD DAY MORE THAN 2,000 YEARS AGO IN SYRACUSE, GREECE, A SHIVERING ARCHIMEDES STEPPED GRATEFULLY INTO A BATHTUB FULL OF HOT WATER. THE TUB HAD BEEN FILLED TO THE BRIM, SO A LOT OF IT SLOSHED OUT ON ALL SIDES WHEN ARCHIMEDES GOT IN. HE HAD HARDLY LOWERED HIMSELF INTO THE TUB AND BEGUN TO ENJOY HIS SOAK WHEN HE SUDDENLY REALIZED WHAT IT ALL MEANT—THE WEIGHT OF THE WATER THAT HAD SPILLED OUT WAS EXACTLY THE SAME AS THE WEIGHT OF THE OBJECT (HIMSELF!) THAT HAD GOT IN! WITH A TRIUMPHANT YELL, ARCHIMEDES JUMPED OUT OF HIS BATH AND RAN NAKED THROUGH THE STREETS OF SYRACUSE TO SHARE HIS DISCOVERY, YELLING 'EUREKA! EUREKA!' ('I FOUND IT! I FOUND IT!'). NOW YOU KNOW WHO WAS RESPONSIBLE FOR CONDEMNING ALL SCIENTISTS TO BEING CALLED 'ABSENT-MINDED'!

END OF STORY. LET'S GO BACK NOW TO BUOYANCY, THE UPWARDS FORCE THAT EXISTS IN ALL FLUIDS. IF THE WEIGHT OF THE OBJECT WHICH IS SUBMERGED IN THE FLUID IS LESS THAN THE WEIGHT OF THE FLUID IT HAS DISPLACED, BUOYANCY WILL BE SO STRONG THAT THE OBJECT WILL FLOAT ON THE SURFACE OF THE FLUID. AND THAT'S WHY YOUR BOTTLE FLOATS ON THE SURFACE OF THE POOL: THE AIR IN IT WEIGHS LESS THAN THE AMOUNT OF WATER DISPLACED BY THE BOTTLE!

EXACTLY THE SAME THING HAPPENS WHEN YOU HOLD THE STRING OF

A HELIUM BALLOON, EXCEPT THAT INSTEAD OF SITTING AT THE BOTTOM OF A POOL OF WATER ABOUT 4 FT DEEP, YOU ARE STANDING AT THE BOTTOM OF A 'POOL' OF AIR SEVERAL KILOMETRES DEEP. THE BALLOON FLOATS UP AS FAR AS THE STRING ALLOWS IT TO BECAUSE THE HELIUM INSIDE IT IS LIGHTER THAN THE AIR DISPLACED BY THE BALLOON.

THE AIR THAT SURROUNDS THE EARTH IS MADE UP MOSTLY OF— SURPRISE! SURPRISE!— NITROGEN, AND NOT OXYGEN OR CARBON DIOXIDE, AS YOU MIGHT HAVE THOUGHT. NITROGEN IS FAR HEAVIER THAN HELIUM, WHICH MAKES AIR IN GENERAL HEAVIER THAN HELIUM.*

AND THAT'S WHY YOU SHOULD NOT LET GO OF THE STRING OF YOUR HELIUM BALLOON.

*Hydrogen is even lighter than helium, so balloons can also be filled with hydrogen if you want them to float. But hydrogen is highly inflammable (it catches fire and explodes at the smallest provocation) so it's always safer to use helium instead.

The real reason why Archimedes ran naked through the streets

WHAT IF THE DINOSAURS CAME BACK?

Oooh, exciting thought! Pretty scary, too. We would all be living in *Jurassic Park* all the time with T-Rexes running amuck and Velociraptors coming after us in savage packs! But there would be good stuff too. Maybe you could go to school on an Apatosaurus—the rest of the traffic would quickly get out of the way—or have a pet Nemicolopterus (a pigeon-sized pterosaur) flying about your room.

Let's pause here for a moment, for an important clarification. Sure the T-Rexes and the Stegosauruses and the Triceratopses became extinct around 65 million years ago, but there was one small sub-group of dinosaurs that did NOT. We still have their descendants living amongst us and we call them...BIRDS! Yes, birds evolved from flying dinosaurs, and scientists are still trying to figure out how these flying dinosaurs were spared the Great Extinction.

So, in that sense, the question 'What if the dinosaurs came back?' is in itself somewhat inaccurate, because really, some of them never went away.

OKAY, LET'S CHANGE THE QUESTION. WHAT IF JURASSIC PARK BECAME A REALITY?

Is there any one of us who would *not* want to see real dinosaurs in the flesh? Not while being torn apart by them, of course, but only SEE them, in all their gigantic glory? Probably not. But here is the sad truth: dinos are not coming back. Not now, not ever. And no, we can't create them in a lab, like they did in the movie *Jurassic Park*, either.

Why? We don't have any dinosaur DNA, that's why!

Now what is DNA? DNA is a molecule that is found in every cell (a few exceptions exist) of every living organism. It has the entire encyclopaedia of instructions for how the organism looks, grows and behaves. This encyclopaedia is passed on from generation to generation, so that the new organism looks and functions very much like its parents. Without this ENTIRE encyclopaedia— which is called a genome—it is impossible to recreate the original organism.

If every cell of an organism has DNA, then surely bones should have it too? And we have found plenty of fossilized dinosaur bones over the years. Shouldn't we be able to extract the DNA from them? Well, theoretically, yes, but even DNA comes with an expiry date. It is a resilient thing, DNA, and can stay viable for—hold your breath— a million years or so, but hey, it has been 65 million years since the very last dinosaur died! A little too late now to start looking for intact dino DNA, don't you think?

Let's say that we did, by some miracle, find a bit of dino genome, but with a few 'pages' missing. In *Jurassic Park*, scientists do find bits of dinosaur DNA, and they do this by extracting dinosaur blood from a mosquito that had got trapped in amber and died just after biting a dinosaur. They reconstruct the missing bits in the DNA (the missing pages in the encyclopaedia) with bits of frog DNA (since dinosaurs were reptiles, just like frogs are, the movie scientists figured that the two must have quite similar info in their DNA). But that is Hollywood, and anything can happen in the movies. In reality, mixing up the DNA of two organisms may result in a third, different organism or *nothing at all*. It certainly would not create a perfect dinosaur. So that route is also closed to us.

What if we found the entire dino genome: a molecule of DNA containing ALL the instructions required to build a new dinosaur? We would STILL have a big problem. We would have to implant this genome into a living egg, so that it could develop into a dinosaur. But what egg would we use? In the movie, the scientists implant the dinosaur DNA into a crocodile egg. In reality, though, this would not work. To 'clone' an animal—that is, to create it in a laboratory—we still need an egg from the same species to implant the genome into. Last time we looked, there were no usable dinosaur eggs lying around anywhere. So that's another dead end.

BIRDS ARE THE ONLY DINOS THAT WERE SMART ENOUGH TO SURVIVE? SO THEY AREN'T REALLY 'BIRD BRAINS', ARE THEY?

Aww, don't look so sad. There's one tiny shred of hope. The big guys may never return, but scientists have had some success with creating a 'dino-chicken'. You see, birds, being descendants of the dinosaurs, still carry bits of dinosaur DNA in them. Only, evolution has suppressed some bits of that DNA to help them fly and feed more easily. That's why birds today have beaks, wings and tail feathers, where they once had teeth, forelimbs and tails. (Ever notice how, apart from human beings, birds are the only creatures that walk on two legs? Just like some dinosaurs did?)

Using biotechnology to 'reawaken' the suppressed genes, scientists have been partly successful in growing chickens with teeth. They are now trying to turn the tail feathers back into tails, and wings into forelimbs. In a couple of decades, we might even be ordering tandoori dino-chicken at the local takeaway!

WHY YOU SHOULD NOT LOSE SLEEP OVER THE RETURN-OF-THE-DINOSAURS NIGHTMARE

Do you really think that we humans, with our advanced, evolved brains and our superior killing machines, would not be able to take on a bunch of gigantic and dangerous, but essentially small-brained reptiles that evolved almost 150 million years before we did? Chances are WE'd end up making THEM extinct. Again.

Well, maybe not completely extinct. Our human curiosity and fascination with dinosaurs would not let that happen. We'd probably keep a few specimens safely locked away in zoos for our fellow men to enjoy, and a few in remote laboratories for our scientists to experiment on. And if we discovered that the Diplodocus could be turned into yummy steaks and kebabs, we'd even breed them for slaughter.

But it would be difficult for the poor dinosaurs to cope with our world today, and we're not even talking of cities and skyscrapers. The earth itself has changed so much in the last 100

million years that the dinosaurs would find it hard to recognize it as their once-happy home.

For one thing, the supercontinent of Pangaea, on which the dinosaurs first evolved, has broken apart, its pieces drifting away from each other to form the continents we know today. In fact, the landmass that we call India collided with the landmass of Asia, forming the Himalayas, some 30 million years AFTER the dinosaurs had become extinct!

The weather has changed considerably too. It was much hotter and more humid when the giant reptiles roamed the earth. There are millions of strange new germs now that their bodies have no idea how to fight. The food they were used to is no longer around. The carnivores would perhaps be okay: a T-Rex would be as happy eating an elephant as an Apatosaurus. But the herbivores would have some trouble, because their digestive systems are just not designed to digest grass. You see, grass only evolved after the dinosaurs had become extinct!

WHAT IF A GIANT X-CLASS SOLAR FLARE HEADED TOWARDS THE EARTH?

Ouch.

But the news is not ALL bad.

The good news first. Bodily harm to human beings will be very limited, for two reasons. One, the blanket of air around the earth that we call the atmosphere will protect us. Two, the earth's magnetic field will repel most of the particles that the solar flare tries to ram into us. A word of caution here: to be protected–really protected–you must be down here, on the surface of the earth. The 'safe from solar flares' guarantee does not apply to airline passengers and astronauts.

The bad news? We live in the twenty-first century, the brave new age of electric power and telecommunications. For that reason, and that reason only, things could get catastrophic for years if the sun decided to send a particularly powerful solar flare in our direction. In fact, if this was the nineteenth century, we would not have had to worry about solar flares at all.

OH REALLY? SO SOLAR FLARES ARE A RECENT THING?

Not at all. It's our technology that is a recent thing. And that is the real problem. Solar flares cannot hurt us, but they can certainly fry all our technology and send us back into, quite literally, the Dark Ages.

You see, solar flares are giant explosions on the sun's surface that release energy equivalent to tens of millions of nuclear bombs. They have been occurring ever since the sun was formed. The earth has lived quite companionably with these 'sun eruptions' for some 4.5 billion years, ever since it was first formed. All life on earth evolved while the sun was merrily shooting off flares in every direction. So really, life on earth has nothing to fear from solar flares.

What has changed in the last 150 years or so, however, is the amount of technology humans have begun to use. All of which began when human beings figured out how to create electricity in a laboratory.

Let's pause briefly here for an important clarification. Electricity was not 'invented' by man. It has always been around in nature: in lightning, in electric eels and some fish, and yes, in solar storms. What man did achieve was this: he studied electricity in nature, figured out how it worked, discovered a way to create it artificially, and then thought of ways to use it to make life easier for himself. This earth-shattering (figuratively speaking) discovery has had a GINORMOUS impact on the world.

Think about it. Until 1836, when the electrical telegraph was invented to instantly send messages over long distances over a wire, electricity had NEVER been used to make something that was useful to humans. Once the telegraph was invented, things really took off. In 1870, Thomas Edison invented the electric bulb, and the world had a way to safely light up (gas lights, which were used for lighting up streets and homes before bulbs, were notorious fire hazards). Over the next 100 years, an incredible number of new inventions that would not have been possible without electricity changed the way we live, work, play, eat and travel forever.

Which is all wonderful, except when an extra powerful X-Class solar flare comes calling. Because when it does, our brilliant man-made electricity-based technologies—everything from refrigerators, elevators computers cell phones, music systems, televisions, microwave ovens and modern automobiles to petrol stations (you need to pump the petrol out, don't you?), medical equipment, air-conditioners, amusement park rides, water filtration systems, industrial machinery, aircraft, satellites, and GPS systems could all get totally fried. In minutes, humanity would zoom back in time to the nineteenth century.

How come a solar storm can disrupt electricity-based technologies so badly? Because when a solar flare erupts, it ejects a giant wave of electricity into space. This electricity interferes with the earth's magnetism, creating what is called a geomagnetic storm.

Geomagnetic storms could jam communication signals (think radio signals and radar signals going haywire, knocking man-made satellites out of orbit and crashing planes) and navigation systems (think completely scrambled GPS), and send phantom electricity surging through transmission grids and transformers, causing them to melt and warp and cut off electricity to entire continents. If the damage is bad enough, it may take YEARS to get those systems up and running again!

Plus, there will be some loss or damage to human life too—people hooked up to life-support equipment will die immediately, others will die later as food supplies and clean water gets affected. Fast-moving particles in the solar wind could pass through the bodies of astronauts and airline passengers, causing damage to body parts, and in some cases, death.

So yes, it wouldn't be pretty. Except for the 'auroras'—fabulous light displays caused by the collision of particles in the solar wind with the particles of the earth's atmosphere—that will light up skies all over the world, instead of just at the poles, where auroras usually occur.

WHY YOU SHOULDN'T LOSE SLEEP OVER THE MONSTER SOLAR FLARE NIGHTMARE

Solar flares erupt around cooler, darker areas on the sun's surface called sunspots. Scientists have observed sunspots for some 400 years (a very, very tiny fraction of the sun's life), and we now know that sunspots are not permanent; they appear, disappear, move and change. Observing sunspots helps us to predict 'space weather', which is as important to our well-being as our own earth weather.

Every eleven years, sunspot activity ramps up towards what is called 'solar maximum'. It is during the solar maximum that we can expect more solar flares, and bigger ones too. This year (2013-2014), the sun is at solar maximum in its current cycle.

But we still don't have to worry too much. We have enough telescopes on earth and in outer space that are constantly trained on the sun, watching everything that's going on. And there *is* a lot of activity, with the sun shooting off flares in every direction, but the flares are mostly small A-, B-, and C-class ones. (Solar flares are classified by the letters of the alphabet—the smallest classified flare is an A-class flare, the biggest is a Z-class flare.) A few medium-sized M-class ones go off from time to time. Very rarely do we see a seriously big X-class one. The good part is, we only have to worry when the flare is directed towards us, AND it is an X-20 class flare or above.

If at all a giant solar flare does erupt AND heads in our direction, we will have enough warning, because it will reach the earth's atmosphere only two or three days later. That is enough time to warn astronauts to turn off their electronics and navigation systems and take shelter until the solar wind has passed, to warn planes not to fly, and to warn electric companies to protect their grids. (Just like you put in surge protectors at home to protect your computers and televisions from voltage surges, electric companies have ways to protect their transmission grids.)

Realizing just how much chaos a monster flare could cause on earth, governments are putting scientists to work creating electronic equipment that will not be affected by bad space weather. Sooner rather than later, all electronics will come with solar flare protection.

Of course, it is quite possible that a big solar flare could hit us before we get there. But it is equally likely that it will only be big enough to create some fabulous fireworks in the sky for us.

WHAT IF A SUPERVOLCANO ERUPTED?

Pray it never happens in our lifetimes. Why? Because a supervolcano is TERRIFYING, that's why. The process would start weeks before the actual eruption, with several massive earthquakes and/or giant tsunamis. When the eruption—make that 'supereruption'—actually happened, thousands of tonnes of rock, magma, gases and ash would be blasted into the air in a continuous, unrelenting stream, for up to an entire week! It would go on to include 'continental-scale' devastation (destruction across an entire continent), a 'volcanic winter' that could last several years, and eventually, the extinction of several species, including ours!

BUT ISN'T A SUPERVOLCANO JUST A BIGGER VOLCANO?

In a sense, yes. Like any other volcano, a supervolcano is also an opening, or crack, in the earth's crust through which hot magma, volcanic ash and gases from the mantle of the earth can escape. Like other volcanoes, supervolcanoes are also usually found at places where the earth's tectonic plates (What are they? See the box on page 42) meet or separate. The one difference between the two is just how MEGA everything about a supervolcano is when compared to a plain old volcano.

How mega exactly are we talking about? Let's see.

Remember when a volcano in Iceland erupted in 2010 and flights to and from Europe were cancelled for almost a week? Yes, the volcano with the unpronounceable name: Eyjafjallajökull (say *eya-fyatla-yokutl*). All that disruption of air travel–the biggest since World War II–happened because there was so much ash in the air all over northern Europe that pilots found visibility to be a big problem. Well, Eyjafjallajökull threw up 0.25 km³ *of ejecta (rocks, ash, other matter from inside the mantle), spewed out an ash plume 9 km high, and was classified as a 4 on the Volcanic Explosivity Index (VEI). In comparison, a supervolcano would be classified as 7 or above on the VEI, and would throw up–prepare to wet your pants–up to or over 1000 km³ of ejecta!

Up for more fun facts? Here goes: the May 1980 eruption of Mount St Helens in Washington State in the USA was classified 5 on the VEI. Its ejecta had a volume of a mere 1.2 km³, and its ash plume was 24 km high, but the devastation it caused was mind-boggling. Hundreds of square kilometres were reduced to wasteland, thousands of animals were killed, ash was carried through the air and deposited over eleven states of the USA, and the country suffered a loss of over a billion dollars. Thousands of human lives were saved only because scientists who were studying the volcano had insisted that the authorities close the national park in which Mount St Helens is located to visitors two months earlier, suspecting that an eruption was going to happen soon.

If that is the kind of damage a VEI 5 volcano can do, can you imagine what would happen if a supervolcano erupted? Let's look at what facts we have from the most recent VEI 7 eruption, the largest in recorded history. (It still isn't considered a supervolcano, because its ejecta was way less than the 1000 km³ expected of a supervolcano, but it is the closest we have). It happened in 1815,

---

*0.25 km³ of ejecta means that if you took all the stuff that the volcano spat out and packed it tightly together, it would make a cube 250 m in length, 250 m in breadth, and 250 m high.

with the eruption of Mount Tambora on the island of Sumbawa, Indonesia.

Mount Tambora erupted on the morning of 10 April 1815, with an ear-shattering blast that was heard 2,600 km away, in the islands of Sumatra and beyond. It threw up 160 km^3 (still only a fraction of the 1000 km^3 of ejecta possible in a supereruption) of ejecta, sent an ash plume skyrocketing all the way to the stratosphere (more than 43 km up), and killed 12,000 people instantly.

All vegetation on the island was destroyed. A moderate-sized tsunami, created as a result of the explosion, hit the shores of many Indonesian islands, killing thousands more. Rivers were clogged and polluted and fields were made barren by the coarser ash particles that fell back to earth. The starvation and disease that happened as a result took some 40,000 more lives over the next few months all over Indonesia.

Some 15 million tons of fine ash particles did not fall back to earth. Instead, they hovered in the atmosphere for months and even years after the eruption, dimming the light and heat from the sun. Winds carried these particles as far as North America and Europe. For a whole year, a haze of 'dry fog' hung over these continents, diffusing the sunlight to such an extent that it was possible for people who lived there to look directly at the sun and see sunspots with the naked eye!

Global temperatures dropped. 1816, the year following the eruption, was recorded by meteorologists as the 'Year Without A Summer'. The Indian monsoon was affected for three full years, causing famine and failed harvests all over the country. Ironically, heavy rains in Great Britain, Europe and the USA caused harvests to fail there, leading to the worst famine of the nineteenth century.

Epidemics broke out all over the world. A new and deadly strain of cholera originated in Bengal in 1816 and spread rapidly across the globe. The continuing cold in Europe led to a severe typhus outbreak between 1816 and 1819.

All things considered, the VEI 7 eruption of Mount Tambora

caused between 70,000 and 80,000 deaths and severe environmental damage, global climate change and endless suffering to millions of people.

And all this just from a VEI 7 eruption, not a real 'supervolcano'. Shudder.

WHY YOU SHOULD NOT LOSE SLEEP OVER THE SUPERVOLCANO NIGHTMARE

- The last 'real' supervolcano happened at Toba in Sumatra, Indonesia, 74,000 years ago. Read that as very, very, VERY long ago. It is unlikely that another one like it will happen any time soon.

- One of the biggest hotspots (a region of high volcanic activity that can erupt and create the same effects as a volcano or a supervolcano) that we know of is the Yellowstone National Park in Wyoming, USA. It has produced several supervolcanoes, the last one 640,000 years ago, and is capable of producing several more, what with the vast reservoir of magma just 8 km below it. BUT there are reasons to breathe easy. Somewhat. See, even if the Yellowstone supervolcano actually erupted next year, and terrible, terrible devastation followed, and global climate change happened, and air traffic was affected for months, and global food and drugs supply was affected, the human species would not be destroyed. Not even the human population of the United States would be finished off.

  So it definitely would NOT be an extinction-level event, although millions may die. India herself has 1.2 *billion* people already, so yeah, humans will continue to live and thrive. So that's something to be happy about. Sort of.

- Recently, geologists have discovered that an extinction-level supervolcano is forming some 3,000 km below the Pacific Ocean with two continent-sized blobs of partially melted rock moving towards each other. When they collide, the pressure will be so intense that a supereruption that will destroy all human life will most certainly follow. But don't hold your breath—the collision is only expected to happen in a 100 million years.

THE JIGSAW PUZZLE OF THE EARTH'S CRUST

THE EARTH'S SURFACE, OR CRUST (ALSO CALLED THE LITHOSPHERE), IS MADE UP OF EIGHT BIG (AND A DOZEN SMALL) IRREGULARLY-SHAPED PIECES OF ROCK THAT FIT TOGETHER LIKE A GIANT JIGSAW PUZZLE. THE PIECES FLOAT ON THE SEA OF LIQUID ROCK (ALSO CALLED THE ASTHENOSPHERE) BENEATH THE EARTH'S SURFACE, LIKE A SHEET OF ICE ON THE SURFACE OF A LAKE. THE JIGSAW PIECES OF THE EARTH'S CRUST ARE CALLED TECTONIC PLATES.

TECTONIC PLATES DO NOT HAVE THE SAME THICKNESS THROUGHOUT. THE THICKER, LIGHTER BITS OF A PLATE PROJECT ABOVE THE OCEAN, APPEARING TO US AS LAND (CONTINENTS AND ISLANDS). THE THINNER, DENSER BITS OF THE SAME PLATE BECOME THE OCEAN BED. WHEN CONTINENTS DRIFT APART OR COME TOGETHER, IT IS BECAUSE THE PLATES ON WHICH THEY ARE LOCATED ARE DRIFTING APART OR COMING TOGETHER. THE CONTINENTS WE KNOW TODAY WERE ORIGINALLY PART OF A SUPERCONTINENT CALLED PANGEA WHICH BROKE ALONG PLATE BOUNDARIES AND DRIFTED APART. THIS IS WHY, IF YOU PUSHED ALL THE CONTINENTS TOGETHER AGAIN—GO ON, TRY IT, CUT OUT THE CONTINENTS FROM A WORLD MAP AND PUSH THEM TOGETHER—YOU WILL FIND THAT THEY ALL FIT TOGETHER!

PLATES ARE CONSTANTLY MOVING, ALTHOUGH VERY, VERY SLOWLY—YOU CERTAINLY CANNOT FEEL IT HAPPENING. IN SOME PLACES (CALLED 'ZONES OF DIVERGENCE'), THE PLATES MOVE APART, ALLOWING LIQUID ROCK FROM THE ASTHENOSPHERE TO OOZE UP AND CREATE NEW CRUST. IN OTHER PLACES (CALLED 'ZONES OF CONVERGENCE'), PLATES MOVE TOWARDS EACH OTHER, WITH ONE PLATE DUCKING UNDER THE OTHER AND MELTING, BECOMING PART OF THE ASTHENOSPHERE AGAIN. BECAUSE BOTH THESE THINGS (NEW CRUST BEING FORMED WHILE OLD CRUST IS BEING DESTROYED) ARE HAPPENING AT THE SAME TIME, THE OVERALL

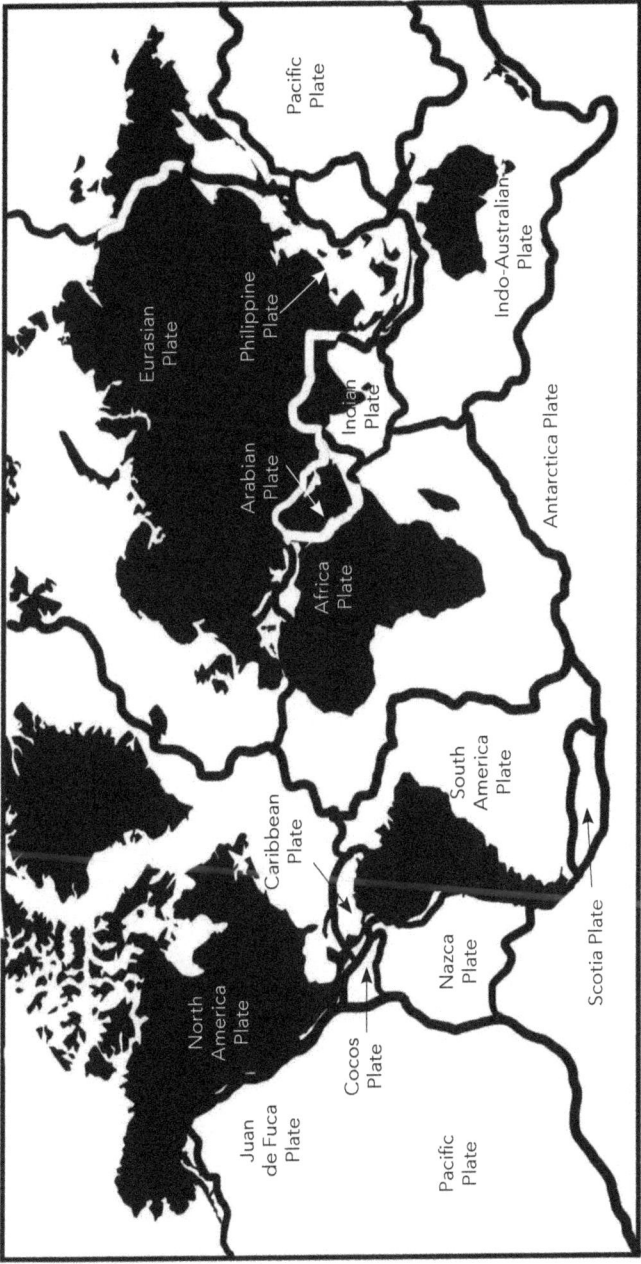

Tectonic plates

AMOUNT OF CRUST REMAINS ROUGHLY THE SAME.

SOMETIMES, THE PLATES JUST SLIP AND SLIDE AGAINST EACH OTHER TOO. WHEN THE MOVEMENT IS SUDDEN, IT CAUSES THINGS ON THE SURFACE TO TOPPLE AND FALL. WE CALL THE EVENT AN EARTHQUAKE. EARTHQUAKES AND VOLCANOES MOST OFTEN HAPPEN AT ZONES OF CONVERGENCE, BECAUSE OF THE PRESSURE CREATED BY ONE PLATE BEING PUSHED UNDER THE OTHER.

WHAT IF THE MAYAN CALENDAR WAS JUST A BIT OFF, AND THE WORLD ACTUALLY ENDS SOMETIME THIS YEAR?

You do know about the rumour that had everyone scared out of their minds in 2012, don't you? The one that said the world was going to end on 21 Dec 2012, because an ancient calendar put together by people from a civilization called the Maya ended on that very same day?

Right. Let us tell you right at the beginning why you shouldn't lose sleep over this one. The world isn't going to end because of what the Mayan calendar said, even if its calculations were a bit off.

Nope, we are not pooh-poohing Mayan mathematicians and astronomers, who were in fact some of the brightest chaps ever to walk the Middle Americas. We are only thumbing our noses at the rumour-mongers who started this whole scare about the world ending on the day the Mayan calendar ended. The bald truth is this—whoever started that rumour does not understand how the Mayan calendar works at all.

FIRST THINGS FIRST. WHO WERE THE MAYA PEOPLE?

The Mayas were a highly developed civilization that occupied and ruled a large area of Central America (southern Mexico, Guatemala, Belize, and parts of Honduras, El Salvador and the Yucatan Peninsula) for almost 4,000 years—from around 2600 BC all the way to the early sixteenth century—until invading Spanish armies seized their land and colonized it. They were the only civilization anywhere on the two great continents of North and South America that had a fully developed written language before the sixteenth century.

The Mayas reached the height of their progress between AD 250 and AD 900. While agriculture was their main occupation, a lot of Mayas lived in large cities, and traded cacao (yes, the beans which give us chocolate!), salt, seashells, gemstones like jade, and a volcanic glass called obsidian which was excellent for making arrowheads, sword blades and decorative objects like plates and trays. They built huge monuments—stepped pyramids for religious ceremonies, highly decorated palaces for their kings—and left long, detailed records of their rulers' achievements on stone slabs in the elaborate script that they had developed. They were excellent mathematicians and astronomers, and had figured out the concept of zero by themselves, as far back as 36 BC.

The Maya civilization began to collapse around 900 AD. One of the theories is that this happened because of overcrowding—at one time, their population numbered in the millions—and the destruction of their own immediate environment through overfarming and overhunting of big animals. We don't know for sure because most of the written records maintained by generations of Mayas were destroyed some 600 years later by intolerant Spanish Catholic priests who believed they were the work of the devil. Sigh.

HOW DID THE MAYAN CALENDAR WORK?

Ah, good question. It is a little complicated to explain, so pay attention now.

Just like we have calendars that have a 7-day weekly cycle, a 28- to 31-day monthly cycle, and a 365- to 366-day yearly cycle, the Mayans also had calendars made up of several cycles of different lengths. The smaller cycles were the 13-day Trecena and the 20-day Winal, the longer ones were the 260-day Tzolk'in and the 365-day Haab'. 52 Haab'—or 73 Tzolk'in—taken together was called the Calendar Round.

This 52-Haab cycle (or in our terms, 52-year cycle, since a Haab' also has 365 days) was a very important unit of time, but since this cycle could only repeat ONCE during a person's lifetime (very few people live beyond 104 years), the Mayas had a different calendar for recording history. This was called the Long Count Calendar. Each cycle on the Long Count Calendar was 13 B'ak'tuns (to know what a B'ak'tun is, see page 48) or about 5,129 years long.

The Mayas believed, like the Hindus, that the world is 'refreshed' or 'recreated' over and over again. Each cycle on the Long Count Calendar begins from the date that the Mayas believed that the world is re-created. The last Mayan Long Count cycle began on 11 August 3114 BC of our modern calendar.

And the last day of that Long Count cycle, according to our calendar, was—you guessed it—21 Dec 2012!

So this is what people figured: if the world had to be 'recreated' afresh the next day, the world would obviously have to be destroyed first. And that would most probably happen on the last day of that cycle, i.e. Dec 21! Everyone began panicking like Chicken Little, conveniently ignoring the fact that the Mayas, while they were smart guys and all, were not exactly divine oracles who could see 5,129 years into the future.

Plus, as Maya experts never tired of telling anyone who would care to listen, the Mayas never said anything about the world being destroyed. For them, the end of one Long Count cycle just meant that a new cycle was beginning. Saying that it meant the end of the world is like saying that the world will end on 31 December each year because a new calendar cycle starts the next day!

Silly, right? So don't worry about the Mayan calendar any more. Just celebrate the beginning of a new Long Count cycle!

GETTING DOWN AND DIRTY WITH THE LONG COUNT CALENDAR

WANT TO REALLY, REALLY UNDERSTAND HOW THE LONG COUNT CALENDAR WORKS? WELL, HERE GOES!

YOU KNOW HOW OUR MODERN NUMBER SYSTEM WORKS, RIGHT? IT IS WHAT WE CALL A DECIMAL SYSTEM OR A 'BASE 10' SYSTEM. THIS MEANS THAT 10 UNITS MAKE 1 TEN, 10 TENS MAKE 1 HUNDRED, 10 HUNDREDS MAKE 1 THOUSAND, AND SO ON. WELL, THE MAYA CALENDAR USED A 'BASE 20' SYSTEM.

1 K'IN = 1 DAY

20 K'IN = 1 WINAL (20 DAYS, ALMOST A MONTH).

18 WINALS = 1 TUN (360 DAYS, ALMOST A YEAR)

20 TUNS = 1 K'ATUN (7200 DAYS = 20 YEARS APPROX)

20 KA'TUNS = 1 B'AK'TUN (144,000 DAYS = 394 YEARS APPROX)

20 B'AK'TUNS = 1 PIKTUN (2,880,000 DAYS = 7,885 YEARS APPROX)

AND SO ON.

(THE ONLY THING THAT DOESN'T FIT IN THIS LONG COUNT CALENDAR IS THAT 18 WINALS, AND NOT 20, MAKE 1 TUN. WHY 18? MAYAN ASTRONOMERS KNEW THAT A 'SOLAR YEAR'—THE TIME TAKEN FOR THE EARTH TO COMPLETE ONE REVOLUTION OF THE SUN—WAS 365 K'INS, SO THEY USED 18, BECAUSE THAT MADE THE LENGTH OF A TUN 360 DAYS, QUITE CLOSE TO THE LENGTH OF THE SOLAR YEAR.)

BET YOU'RE THINKING THAT THE LONG COUNT CALENDAR MUST HAVE BEEN HUMUNGOUS. SURPRISINGLY, IT WASN'T! THE MAYAS HAD A NIFTY LITTLE DEVICE TO KEEP TRACK OF THEIR K'INS AND TUNS. IT WAS VERY LIKE A CAR ODOMETER, WHICH KEEP TRACK OF THE DISTANCE YOU TRAVEL. IN AN ODOMETER, THE RIGHTMOST COLUMN OF NUMBERS

MOVES THE FASTEST, COUNTING UP BY ONE EVERY TIME YOU TRAVEL 100 METRES. ONCE 1,000 METRES (1 KM) HAVE BEEN TRAVELLED, THE RIGHTMOST COLUMN RESETS TO 0 AND THE COLUMN TO ITS LEFT GOES UP BY 1. ONCE THIS SECOND COLUMN GOES UP TO 9, IT IN TURN RESETS TO 0 AND THE COLUMN NEXT TO IT GOES UP BY 1. IT'S VERY SIMILAR TO THE PLACE VALUE SYSTEM YOU LEARN IN MATHS.

IF YOUR CAR HAS TRAVELLED 12,235 KMS AND 700 M IN THE LAST TWO YEARS, FOR INSTANCE, YOUR CAR ODOMETER WILL READ LIKE THIS:

CAR ODOMETER

TEN THOUSANDS (KM)	THOUSANDS (KM)	HUNDREDS (KM)	TENS (KM)	UNITS (KM)	100 METRES
1	2	2	3	5	7

THE ONLY DIFFERENCE WITH THE MAYAN 'ODOMETER' IS THAT IT IS A BASE 20 DEVICE. ON THE DAY BEFORE THE WORLD WAS CREATED, THE MAYAN 'ODOMETER', ACCORDING TO THE MAYANS, LOOKED LIKE THIS:

MAYAN LONG COUNT CALENDAR:DAY BEFORE CREATION

B'AK'TUNS	KA'TUNS	TUNS	WINALS	K'INS
13	0	0	0	0

THE NEXT DAY, ON 11 APRIL 3114 BC, A FRESH TIME CYCLE BEGAN, AND THE 'ODOMETER' RESET TO:

0.0.0.0.0

AND A NEW CYCLE, STARTING FROM THE 'DAY OF CREATION', BEGAN. THE K'INS STARTED COUNTING UP ON THE RIGHTMOST COLUMN, LIKE THIS.

0.0.0.0.1 (1 DAY)

0.0.0.0.2 (2 DAYS)

0.0.0.0.3 (3 DAYS)

....

0.0.0.0.19 (19 DAYS)

AFTER THIS POINT, SINCE 1 WINAL WOULD BE COMPLETE THE NEXT DAY, THE LONG COUNT CALENDAR CHANGED TO:

(20 DAYS = 1 WINAL)

OVER THE NEXT 20 K'INS, THE ODOMETER WENT ON TO READ:

0.0.0.1.1 (21 DAYS)

0.0.0.1.2 (22 DAYS)

....

0.0.0.1.19 (39 DAYS)

0.0.0.2.0 (40 DAYS = 2 WINALS)

ON THE DAY BEFORE 18 WINALS OR 1 TUN WAS COMPLETED, THE CALENDAR READ:

0.0.0.17.19 (17 X 20 + 19 = 359 DAYS)

AND THE NEXT DAY, IT READ:

0.0.1.0.0 (360 DAYS = 1 TUN)

NOW THAT 1 TUN WAS DONE, THE NEXT BIG CHANGE WOULD COME WHEN 1 KA'TUN WAS DONE. THE DAY BEFORE 20 TUNS ENDED, THE CALENDAR READ:

0.0.19.17.19 (19 X 360 + 17 X 20 + 19 = 7,199 DAYS)

AND THE NEXT DAY, WHEN 1 KA'TUN WAS COMPLETED, IT READ:

0.1.0.0.0 (7,200 DAYS = 1 KA'TUN)

SIMILARLY, ON THE DAY BEFORE 1 B'AK'TUN WAS COMPLETED, THE CALENDAR READ:

0.19.19.17.19 (19 X 7,200 + 19 X 360 + 17 X 20 + 19 = 143,999 DAYS)

AND THE NEXT DAY, OF COURSE:

1.0.0.0.0 (144,000 DAYS = 1 B'AK'TUN)

NOW COMES THE EXCITING BIT. TAKE A LOOK AT THE CALENDAR A DAY BEFORE THE 13 B'AK'TUNS WERE COMPLETED.

12.19.19.17.19 (1,871,999 DAYS)

AND NOW—HOLD YOUR BREATH!—HERE'S HOW THE CALENDAR LOOKED THE NEXT DAY.

13.0.0.0.0 (1,872,000 DAYS)

YES, THE CALENDAR LOOKED EXACTLY AS IT DID THE DAY BEFORE THE MAYAN CREATION OF THE WORLD, INDICATING THAT THE NEXT LONG COUNT CYCLE WAS NOW READY TO BEGIN. COOL, HUH?

WHAT IF ROBOTS TOOK OVER THE WORLD?

Let's rephrase that question a little before we begin to think of the answers. Actually, let's ask three completely different questions and try and answer them first.

1. What do you imagine when you hear the word robot?
2. What is a robot, actually?
3. Aren't robots taking over the world already?

ANSWER 1:

If you are like most people and watch a lot of movies and TV shows, you probably imagine a robot as an android: a machine that looks and acts like a human. Except that it moves jerkily (like Michael Jackson), has a flat expressionless voice and has eyes that flash when it is turned 'on'. (Okay, maybe not exactly that but something close to it.) In our minds, a robot is one of two things: a) an uncomplaining, obedient slave, helping us with our homework, cleaning up our rooms in a flash, helping our team win the basketball match; or b) a terrifying enemy: a superior but emotionless 'machine intelligence' that will go rogue at some point, clone itself into a massive unstoppable army of its likenesses (remember the Rajnikanth movie *Robot*), and destroy us all.

ANSWER 2:

The actual 'definition' of a robot, however, is quite different. A robot is 'any electro-mechanical machine that is guided by a computer program or electronic circuits.' Such robots don't look anything like we imagine them to be; many of them are just mechanical arms that can perform a repetitive task thousands of times with far more accuracy and speed than any human. Some of them are vehicles that can traverse a track over and over again without ever whining that they're bo-o-o-red.

ANSWER 3:

Yes, robots are already taking over the world! They are *everywhere*, only you don't know it. They are:

- in car factories: welding, gluing and painting car parts along the assembly line;
- in warehouses: lifting heavy goods and moving them from one location to another;
- in packaging units: picking juice cartons off a conveyor belt and stacking them neatly in boxes;
- in orchards and fields: picking vegetables and fruit;
- in hospital operating rooms: camouflaged as tiny cameras that enter your intestines and arteries;
- in our homes: vacuuming our floors,
- in our computers: beating us at chess, talking to us through our smartphones and GPS systems, finding in milliseconds the one page we are looking for out of the millions on the world wide web.

Robots boldly go where no human has gone before, into the farthest reaches of the solar system and the deepest trenches on the ocean floor. They go into situations and places dangerous for humans—minefields, war zones, nuclear radiation zones and more.

THE BOT FUTURE: THE GOOD, THE BAD AND THE SCARY

Overall, robots are helping us live longer, healthier, safer and easier lives. The trouble is, they can also be trained to destroy, pollute and kill, and they will do these jobs just as quickly and accurately as they do others. What's even scarier is that they will do them unquestioningly and emotionlessly. NOT a comforting thought.

There is no way around that one though. We are already severely dependent on robots, and cannot wish them away. In fact, as time goes by, more and more of them will join the workforce, each one doing the work of ten humans or more, never asking for salaries, food or friends. Robots will not bunk work, fall ill, get bored or complain. They will be every employer's dream employees.

But, you say anxiously, what will happen to US then? As robots take over our factories and warehouses and schools and offices, thousands and thousands of humans will lose their jobs! There will be huge riots, violence, hunger, disease, death!

Relax! The last time this happened was 200 years ago, during the Industrial Revolution, when machines for spinning, weaving, paper making, ploughing, harvesting, and much more were invented. 70 per cent of the workforce lost their jobs. Machine-haters called Luddites even went after the 'metal monsters' that stole their jobs with huge sledgehammers. The result? A few machines were destroyed, but machines didn't go away from our lives. Neither did they take over the world and kill off the humans they replaced.

On the contrary, machines just made our lives simpler. They freed us up from hard, exhausting physical work and gave us time to think about what we *really* wanted to do. They gave us the freedom to become dancers and musicians and artists, and they created new kinds of jobs for humans, the kind they could not have imagined before the machines came.

Another kind of Industrial Revolution—the Information Revolution—arrived recently, with computers and technology.

Once again, new, sophisticated machines began doing our jobs for us,except this time they were doing jobs we use our BRAINS for, not our hands.

For now, technology, like the machines of the first Industrial Revolution, has simply made our lives massively better. We have instant access to the entire world's knowledge through the Internet, we can watch the World Cup Football final as it happens from our living rooms, we are seeing and speaking to friends across the planet in real time, *whenever we like*. Technology has also created its own new jobs: software programmer, web developer, graphic designer, visual effects (VFX) artist, and hundreds more;jobs that your grandparents could not have imagined would ever exist.

What will happen when robots get as smart as humans is impossible to predict, but the good news (or the bad news, depending on how you look at it) is that we are still not quite sure IF these machines will ever get there.

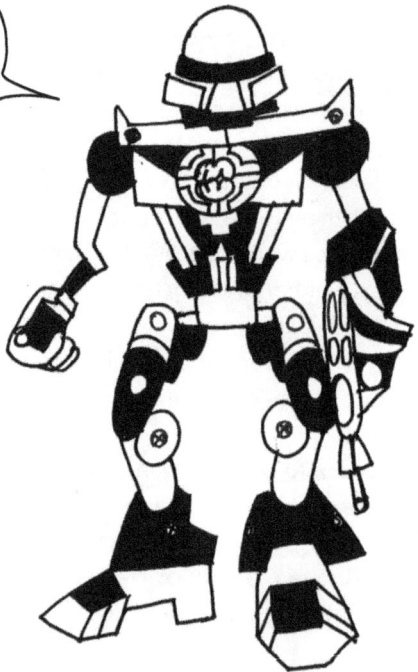

SEVEN BILLION HUMANS DOWN, ONE TO GO. NOW WHERE IS THE ONE THEY CALL RAJNIKANTH?

WHY YOU SHOULDN'T LOSE SLEEP OVER THE KILLER BOTS NIGHTMARE

First of all, refer to the para above. We are not quite sure if we can ever create robot 'brains' that have the same power and complexity as the human brain. Phew.

However, some scientists and futurists are pretty confident that robots that can 'think' are just around the corner (in the next twenty to thirty years, tops), and that does sound a little scary. Robots can already calculate, read truckloads of information in a jiffy, and memorize things way, wayyyy better and faster than we can (a robot called Watson recently read every single Wikipedia page in two weeks, and has enough memory in its hard disk to remember ALL of that information, forever!); if they also begin to 'think', they will almost certainly become 'superhuman'.

That would be the end of us, wouldn't it? Once the 'superhuman' robots realize that we humans are of little use to them, they will surely kill us off, just like we kill off ants and mosquitoes.

Well, that *could* happen, of course, but sadly, what we *really* should be worried about is not the robots themselves, but the small, elite, wealthy, powerful group of *humans who own, or will own, the robots*. With their superhuman robots to make their lives easier, they may decide to turn the rest of us into slaves or eliminate us altogether.

The truth is, no machine yet invented can beat us humans in our capacity for selfishness and greed. And THAT'S the really scary part.

But it is also true that no machine yet invented has the enormous human capacity for love, kindness and intelligence. So maybe it will all work out okay in the end—maybe the elite humans will decide to spare us, or maybe all humans will work together to ensure that the robots NEVER get the better of us.

Now hold that lovely thought, and go to sleep...

WHAT IF THE EARTH STOPPED SPINNING?

Don't even think about it. It's a truly, truly scary thought.

Why? Consider this. You are travelling in a car that's being driven by a maniacal speed demon. The speedometer is inching towards the land speed record of 1,227.99 kms per hour (currently held by Andy Green of the UK's Royal Air Force, driving a Thrust supersonic car, the first car to achieve a speed faster than the speed of sound.)

Suddenly, a big obstacle rears up ahead of you. In the nanosecond between the driver slamming the brakes and you sailing through the windshield headfirst at almost the speed of sound, one thought flashes like lightning through your brain: Uh oh. I should have worn my seatbelt.

Now consider this. You are actually in a moving vehicle right now, but you probably don't realize that it is even moving because it is so BIG. The 'vehicle' is moving way faster than the speed of sound, at some 1,600 km per hour. This 'vehicle' has no seatbelts. And if *this* vehicle should stop moving right now, at this very instant, well...

WHAT WOULD ACTUALLY HAPPEN IF THE EARTH STOPPED SPINNING: A BLOW BY BLOW ACCOUNT

You've probably guessed by now that the 'vehicle' we were

referring to is the earth itself. Since the earth completes one rotation every 24 hours and the diameter of the earth at the Equator is about 40,000 km, we can calculate that the earth's speed of rotation is about 1,650 km per hour.

How would it stop? Let's just suspend our disbelief for a minute and imagine that a giant cosmic hand or something reaches out of the universe and, with one finger, stops the earth ball from rotating. What will happen next?

Here's what:

- Inertia will instantly kick in, and, here comes the scary bit, *send everything and everyone on the earth flying off, at 1,650 km per hour*! (What's inertia? Basically, it is a grand name for the habit of things in the universe to keep moving in the direction they are moving, unless a force from outside of themselves makes them stop or change direction. More details in the box on page 59.)

- Because of inertia, the oceans will continue moving in the direction of the earth's rotation. Can you imagine what will happen when all the water of the oceans slams into every coastline around the world at 1,650 kmph? Only the world's biggest tsunami ever, that's what! At that speed, the water will strip bare all the land it sloshes over.

- The air will continue moving at earth speed too. This supersonic (faster than sound) 'breeze' will crash into trees, homes, highways, dams, cellphone towers and everything else, reducing them to rubble. Yeah, if the water doesn't get you, the wind will.

- But the wind and water can only work on things that are left standing when the earth stops. You certainly won't be. The new supersonic you, like everything else, would have zipped away sideways at enormous speed. You won't fly off into space (for that, you have to be moving at rocket speed, which is over 40,000 kmph) but you will do yourself some very serious damage. Like, erm, instant death.

- What will add to the fun is this: remember how we talked about how the earth is not quite solid all the way through to its core? In fact, the earth's surface, or crust, floats on a hot, molten, liquid underground 'sea'. That 'sea' will also move sideways at 1,650 kmph, and when it does, it will tear the crust apart. Earthquakes galore!

- Of course, this kind of catastrophic stuff will only happen if the earth went from 1,650 kmph to 0 kmph in an instant. If it stopped spinning more slowly, taking a few months or years over it, nothing like this will happen. What will happen then is that our lovely 24-hour day will become a 6-month day! You see, even after the earth stopped rotating, it would continue to revolve around the sun, so every side of the earth would get to see the sun, but only for six months a year.

- With sunlight only for six months, many species of plants and animals would not survive, and our food chain would probably get affected.

- Without rotation, many other changes would happen for reasons that are too complicated to explain here. Some of the changes could be:

  * The land at the north and the south poles would disappear underwater as the water of the world's oceans, kept where they are by rotation, sped away towards the poles.

  * With the oceans gone from around the Equator, there would be a supercontinent there instead, a fat band of land around the centre of the earth, separating a north ocean and a south ocean.

  * The earth's magnetic field would disappear, and with it, our planet's ability to repel all the bad stuff the sun shoots at us all the time. (We don't realize this because the earth's magnetic field shields us so well.)

WHY YOU SHOULDN'T LOSE SLEEP OVER THE NON-SPINNING EARTH NIGHTMARE

THE 'SUDDEN-STOP' SCENARIO:

It will never happen. It *can't*. The laws of physics forbid it. Now smile.

Suppose you have warning that, despite everything, sudden-stop is scheduled for, like, tomorrow, take a flight to Antarctica or the North Pole NOW. The earth's spin-speed is highest at the Equator, and almost zero at the Poles. If you were standing at one of the Poles when the earth stopped spinning, you would not feel it at all!

THE 'GRADUAL-STOP' SCENARIO:

Again, won't happen. Not for billions of years at least, and even then, we are not quite sure that it will.

If it does happen and humans are still around, how bad could it get? Human beings would surely have figured out a way to not only adapt to, but also enjoy, a non-spinning earth, even if it were a very different earth from the one we live on now. So keep calm and eat your doughnut.

WHAT EXACTLY IS INERTIA AGAIN?

THE LAW OF INERTIA, ALSO CALLED ISAAC NEWTON'S FIRST LAW OF MOTION, SAYS THAT A BODY AT REST WILL CONTINUE TO BE AT REST AND A BODY IN MOTION WILL CONTINUE TO BE IN MOTION UNLESS AN EXTERNAL FORCE ACTS UPON IT.

LET'S TRY AND UNDERSTAND WHAT THAT REALLY MEANS. LET'S SAY YOUR SCHOOL BUS IS TRAVELLING AT 50 KM PER HOUR AND THE DRIVER BRAKES SUDDENLY BECAUSE A COW DECIDED TO AMBLE ACROSS THE ROAD. WHAT HAPPENS TO YOU? YOU GET THROWN FORWARD IN YOUR SEAT. AND IF YOU ARE NOT CAREFUL, YOU COULD HURT YOURSELF BY SLAMMING INTO THE SEAT IN FRONT. WHY DOES THAT HAPPEN? BECAUSE OF INERTIA.

SEE, WHEN YOU'RE RIDING IN THE BUS, YOU PROBABLY THINK THAT

YOU ARE JUST SITTING STILL AND IT IS THE BUS THAT IS MOVING FORWARD, BUT THAT IS NOT TRUE. YOUR BODY IS ALSO MOVING FORWARD AT THE SAME SPEED AS THE BUS! SO WHEN THE BUS STOPS SUDDENLY, YOUR BODY CONTINUES MOVING FORWARD AT 50 KM PER HOUR FOR A MILLISECOND OR SO, UNTIL THE EXTERNAL FORCE THAT STOPPED THE BUS ALSO WORKS ON YOUR BODY AND BRINGS IT TO A STOP.

YOU DON'T GET THROWN FORWARD WHEN THE BUS COMES TO A HALT GRADUALLY BECAUSE YOUR BODY IS ALSO SLOWING DOWN GRADUALLY. NOW DO YOU SEE WHY YOUR BUS TEACHER ORDERS YOU TO KEEP SITTING UNTIL THE BUS HAS COME TO A *COMPLETE* STOP? AND WHY YOUR MOM IS ALWAYS YELLING AT YOU FOR NOT WEARING YOUR SEAT BELT? RIGHT! THEY DON'T WANT YOU TO BECOME INERTIA'S NEXT VICTIM, THAT'S ALL.

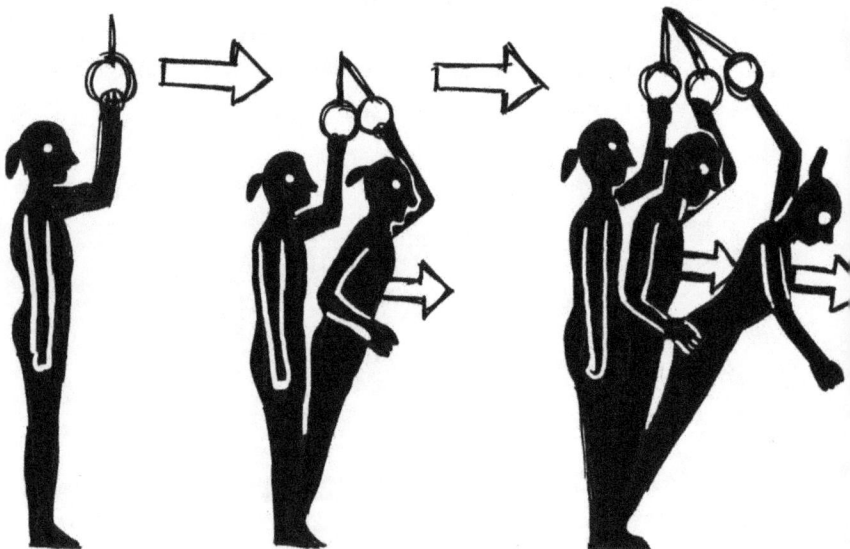

Clear road ahead

Cow steps into the road. Screeech! Bus driver slams the brakes. Your body doesn't.

Squeeeal! Bus comes to a sudden stop. Your body keeps going.

Inertia strikes again!

SECTION II

5 SCIENTIFIC 'FACTS'
THAT YOU SHOULD
STOP BELIEVING

TOILET SEATS ARE THE DIRTIEST SURFACES IN THE HOUSE

Here's a shocker coming right at you: it is probably safer to chop vegetables on your toilet seat than it is to chop them on your kitchen counter or on a chopping board!

And once you've recovered from your dead faint, we'll tell you why.

The short answer to why your toilet seat is cleaner than your kitchen counter is this: BECAUSE you believe that there's nothing dirtier than the toilet seat, you clean it far more often and far more thoroughly than any other surface! The kitchen counter is constantly wiped down too, but not with the kind of strong germ-killing cleaning agents you would use in your bathroom. Also, erm, you wipe the kitchen counter down with a kitchen sponge, which—hold your breath—is by far the dirtiest (read: most germ-infested) thing you have in your house.

But this is too much loose talk in a book on science. Science needs hard numbers, statistics, evidence! Here you go, then: according to a revolutionary study conducted by American microbiologist Dr Charles Gerba of the University of Arizona in 2012, the average number of bacteria per square inch (psi) on a toilet seat is only about 50. Far, far worse is the number of bacteria psi on a kitchen sponge / wiping cloth: 10 million! Even dry dishcloths in the kitchen, which we use to wipe dishes dry, have up to a million bacteria psi!

In fact, Dr Gerba now uses the average number of bacteria on a toilet seat as the *basic unit of measuring how germ-infested a surface is.* For instance, instead of saying that a kitchen sponge has 10 million bacteria psi, he just says it is 200,000 times dirtier than a toilet seat. Which somehow sounds much more shocking.

HUMPH! MY REPUTATION AS THE DIRTIEST THING IN THE HOUSE HAS GONE TO POT!

BUT WHY ARE KITCHEN SPONGES SO FULL OF GERMS?

Well, for one thing, because we just don't wash them very often. Since we are running water over them so many times a day, we don't feel the need to wash them more.

It is also important to understand what KIND of germs we are talking about. Dr Gerba's study looked particularly at–gross-out alert!–faecal bacteria, or bacteria that are found in faeces (also known as potty, shit, crap etc.) These bacteria have exotic names too, like Escherichia coli (or E.coli) and Staphylococcus aureus (both nice names for rock bands, don't you think?).

But how do faecal bacteria get on to kitchen surfaces? (Ewwww!) Sometimes through YOUR HANDS (if you don't wash them well with soap and water and scrub for about 20 seconds every time you use the toilet). But that's not really the main route. You see, millions of E. coli routinely live in the lower intestines of warm-blooded organisms, including ours. While some kinds of E. coli are responsible for causing food poisoning and gastritis, most E. coli are beneficial for us, helping to produce certain vitamins that we need and preventing other disease-causing micro-organisms from taking up residence in our gut.

The E. coli on the kitchen sponge and on our chopping boards comes from the meat that we chop there (remember animal intestines have E. coli too) and from vegetables grown in sewage-contaminated water and/or soil contaminated with animal and human faeces.

An important thing to remember is that E. coli itself isn't a terrible thing to have on your kitchen sponge, because, like we said before, most of them are harmless. But if E. coli, which is, after all, a faecal bacterium, is around, who's to say there aren't other kinds of faecal bacteria around too? Including Extremely Dangerous Guys like salmonella and shigella, which cause dysentery, food poisoning and typhoid!

Speaking of dangerous contamination, another BIG culprit is the reusable shopping bag! Yes, the same jute/cotton/whatever other type of shopping bag you have been virtuously carrying around so that you can avoid using plastic bags. In an interview with BBC News, Dr Gerba revealed this shocking fact: 'Some people have more faecal bacteria in their grocery bag than in their underwear,' he said, 'because at least they wash their underwear!'

In fact, anything that human fingers touch, be it cellphones, light switches, computer keyboards and mice (plural of computer mouse), kitchen and bathroom taps, escalator handrails, banisters of stairways, playground equipment, grocery store trolleys, library books, currency (coins and notes), armrests in movie halls, grip-rails in buses, TV remotes, elevator buttons, is far, far more contaminated with germs than toilet seats are, because human fingers rarely touch toilet seats anyway.

WOW. THEN HOW COME PEOPLE DON'T FALL ILL MORE OFTEN ?

Put that down to two million years of evolution—two million years over which the human body has gotten better and better at building itself an immune system that totally rocks at protecting us from disease.

That doesn't mean you should just sit around feeling smug, though. India is listed as one of the most unhygienic countries in the world, so we have to be extra careful.

But don't go overboard. Human skin is crawling with millions of germs, and many, many of them are good for us. So while you must wash your hands often and well, especially after you have used the toilet and when you come home from school or from the park, don't wash them so often that even your protective germs get washed away. Also, don't use very strong soaps—the chemicals in them could damage your skin and let the germs in. And we all know that our skin—the largest organ in our body—is the first and best barrier against germs.

One last piece of advice from Dr Gerba: close the toilet seat before you flush! It keeps the faecal germs in the bowl! If you don't, the fine spray upwards from the toilet bowl could travel 20 feet in any direction, covering you, your clothes, and—ugh!— your *toothbrush* in tons of faecal bacteria. On aeroplanes, close the bowl AND the toilet door when you flush or you will flood the plane with exotic germs from all over the world.

Oh, and if you want to save yourself all this trouble and all the worry, use Indian-style toilets!

SUGAR MAKES CHILDREN HYPERACTIVE

This is something you've heard forever, haven't you? And from the evidence—your own birthday parties when you were younger, which just got noisier and noisier and wilder and wilder as more sweet things went down the hatch—birthday cake, candy, gulab jamuns, fizzy drinks, cookies—it seems as if the correlation between sugar and hyperactivity is very strong. But here's the fact of the matter: *there is no proven link between the two.*

BUT EVERYONE SAYS IT IS TRUE...AND YOU CAN SEE IT HAPPENING BEFORE YOUR EYES!

Just because people say it is true doesn't automatically make something true. The scientific way to prove that something is true is through observation, experimentation, data collection and analysis. Even though the first part, that is, the observation of children bouncing off the walls in situations where a lot of sugary food and drinks are served, may seem to agree with the hypothesis*, nothing becomes scientific fact until all the other parts of the process are tried and tested.

Many hypotheses (the plural of hypothesis) remain just that until someone decides to investigate it thoroughly to prove

---

*Hypothesis is the scientific word for a statement that is put forward as true, but which still needs to be proved true through rigorous scientific methods.

once and for all whether it is actually true or not. The good part is that, in the case of the 'Sugar Makes Kids Hyper' hypothesis, extensive experiments HAVE actually been done by scientists and laboratories for many years now.

In one of the well-known experiments, the researchers visited a preschool, divided the children into two groups, and handed both groups similar-looking sugary drinks and sweets. Only the researchers knew that one group was eating and drinking food with real sugar in it, while the other was consuming food with an artificial sweetener in it. While their parents watched, researchers tracked the behaviour of the kids in both groups after they had finished their snack. Surprise, surprise! Both groups behaved very similarly: the sugar had not had any effect at all!

In another study, the same thing was done, except that THIS time, the parent accompanying the child was told whether the child was consuming real sugar or artificial sweetener. However, the researchers were not always telling the truth. They told parents whose children were consuming sugar that they were consuming artificial sweetener, and parents whose children were consuming sweetener that they had consumed sugar. Then the researchers sat back and watched, while parents themselves filled in forms reporting their observations on their children's behaviour after the snack.

An interesting result came out of this experiment. Most parents who were made to believe that their kids had consumed sugar reported that their kids were indeed hyperactive after the snack, while other parents, who had been made to believe otherwise, reported that their child's behaviour had not changed much.

> WHAT DO YOU MEAN I CAN'T HAVE MORE CANDY? I THOUGHT LITTLE GIRLS ARE MADE OF SUGAR AND SPICE!

There was a further twist to the tale. Researchers noticed that parents who believed that their children had had sugar watched their kids more closely, scolded them more, and seemed generally more concerned about their behaviour than parents who believed that their children had consumed artificial sweetener!

So actually, sugar DID have an effect on behaviour, but on the *parents'* behaviour, not the children's!

WHY DO LITTLE KIDS GET HYPER AT BIRTHDAY PARTIES, THEN?

Because they are little kids, that's why! First of all, there is the anticipation of going to a birthday party. Once they get there, already hopping with excitement, there are friends waiting, and games, and yummy treats, and possibly a piñata, and a magician, and presents to carry back home as well! Heck, it's enough to make YOU hyper, let alone a little kid!

All the running around and screaming obviously tires little kids out, but they don't realize it, and they don't want to stop running and screaming, so they just keep doing it, running faster and faster until their exhausted little bodies yell for them to stop. But they STILL don't want to stop, so they keep running round the room and jumping off the couch, until, suddenly, the exhaustion really hits them, at which point they get very, very cranky. Sound like your little cousin?

SO LITTLE KIDS SHOULD BE ALLOWED ALL THE SUGAR THEY WANT?

NO! No link has been found between chowing down on sugar and hyperactivity, but there are several other very good reasons why little kids—and even older ones like YOU!—should be allowed only limited amounts of sugar. But if you are too cool to research boring stuff like that, and are happy to live with a mouthful of rotting teeth and weighing scales that have nervous breakdowns every time they see you approach, go on scarfing down that sugar. We aren't so uncool that we'd actually tell you what to do now, would we?

A COIN FALLING ON YOUR HEAD FROM THE 100TH FLOOR OF THE BURJ KHALIFA CAN KILL YOU

Don't get the hard hats out yet if you are planning on visiting the Burj anytime soon. Even if someone accidentally—or deliberately!—drops a coin from the 100th floor, chances are very slim that you will die from the impact of the coin on your head. Be warned, though: if someone decided to drop something else a little heavier and/or shaped differently, the story would not have such a happy ending.

BUT THEN WHY DO SMALL OBJECTS CAUSE SO MUCH DAMAGE WHEN THEY FALL FROM A HEIGHT?

For many different reasons, but mainly because the higher the height that an object falls from, the greater its speed. Why do objects pick up speed, or accelerate, as they fall? Because of the earth's gravity, a super-strong force that pulls them down, down, down. This increase in an object's speed as it plummets towards the earth is called 'Acceleration Due To Gravity', and is usually referred to, in short, as 'g'.

So just how fast does an object accelerate as it heads earthwards? In other words, what is the exact value of 'g'? The answer is 9.81 metres/second squared. Yeah, the 'second-squared' and stuff makes it sound very complicated, but it really isn't. What it means, simply, is that the speed of a free-falling object increases by 9.81 m per second, *every* second. Obviously, the longer an object takes to hit the ground, the higher its speed.

The weight of the falling object also matters. Although the earth pulls at all objects, whether they're big, small, light or heavy with the same force, and although all objects fall with the exact same acceleration of 9.81 m/second squared, the impact that a falling object makes on something below obviously depends on the weight of the object. Heavier objects fall with greater force, and therefore will do greater damage when they fall than lighter objects.

Put these two factors—the weight of an object and the speed at which it is travelling (which in turn depends on the height it is falling from)—together, and it is easy to see that even a small, light object can have quite an impact when it falls a great distance.

In fact, let's calculate how long it will take for a coin to fall from the 100th floor of the Burj Khalifa. Let's say the coin weighs about a gram, and that the 100th floor is about 1,000 feet, or about 300 metres, above the ground. The coin will then reach the ground in a little less than 9 seconds, travelling at about 90 metres per second, or close to 330 km per hour!

Haaaaalp!

HOW COME A COIN TRAVELLING AT THAT SPEED DOESN'T CAUSE THAT MUCH DAMAGE, THEN?

Well, for one thing, because all these calculations of how fast an object falls only consider how hard the earth pulls on an object ('g', in other words) but do not at all consider a very important force that works in the OPPOSITE direction to the earth's pull: air resistance. If an object was falling in a room from which all the air had been sucked out, that is, in vacuum, then 'g' would be the only force, and the object would indeed fall at the speed it is supposed to. But in a real situation, objects fall through air, and the air 'drags' on the falling object, slowing it down. So when the object reaches the earth, it is falling much slower than it is supposed to.

In fact, based on real experiments (do *not* try this at home), we know that a coin falling from the 100th floor will be travelling only at around 45 metres per second (or 160 km per hour) when it reaches the ground, which is very different from the 90 metres per second of the previous calculation.

Also, a coin is not the perfect shape for falling fast through the air, because it is thin and flat. A flat object has more area for the air to drag on. Think of how slowly a leaf falls compared to a seed. A seed falls faster because it has less surface area for the air to drag on, compared to a leaf. Because the coin is also light, apart from being flat, the air flips it over as it falls, slowing it down even further and even carrying it away for a distance. The coin would most likely land somewhere else, not even directly below where it was dropped.

With how much impact-force would this coin hit you? Less than 1 foot-pound (1 foot-pound is the energy required to lift a 450 gm weight 1 foot off the ground). All things considered, that is a very small impact force. (The minimum impact-force needed to crack a human skull is estimated at 100 foot-pounds.)

So if you do indeed happen to be standing under the Burj Khalifa nine seconds after someone dropped a coin from the

100th floor, AND the coin does strike your head, don't worry; the coin won't even hurt you, let alone kill you.

PHEW. BUT WHAT IF A PEN WERE DROPPED INSTEAD?

Now you're talking! If someone on the 100th floor of the Burj decided to drop a metal-cased fountain pen weighing about 50 gm instead of a coin, you'd better get out of the way fast!

The fountain pen's weight (50 times the weight of our coin) and long, slim 'aerodynamic' shape (an aerodynamic shape attracts far less air resistance than a non-aerodynamic shape) will make it fall straight to earth like an arrow, at some 400 km per hour, giving it an impact-force of 100 foot-pounds, which could most definitely crack your skull. You may survive given that the air resistance will slow the pen down some, but you would be badly hurt.

So do pack that hard-hat before you get on that plane to Dubai. Just in case.

YOUR FINGERNAILS AND HAIR WILL CONTINUE TO GROW EVEN AFTER YOU'RE DEAD

As she crested the hill on her way home from school that day, Vittie shivered a little. She should not have waited so late for the stranger on the phone to show up at the café, she shouldn't. But what he had promised to show her had sounded so incredible, so intriguing, so life-altering, that she had been loath to pass it up entirely. Then he hadn't arrived, of course. Perhaps she had always known that he wouldn't.

Now dusk had fallen, and a slight breeze, rather more chilly than usual for this time of the year, had picked up. Clouds scudded across the night sky, obscuring the pale sliver of moon. The tamarinds bordering the old cemetery groaned and creaked as they swayed, reaching for something she couldn't see with dark, grasping fingers.

Vittie quickened her steps, her breath coming fast and shallow. If she could only get past the cemetery without freaking out completely, she would be fine. She could already see the lights of her village at the bottom of the hill. Just another hundred metres to safety. She kept her eyes on the ground and upped her pace a notch. She had this.

Past the first gate of the cemetery now: yessss! One step at a time... Keep going. Keep going. She cursed the roots of the tamarinds under her breath. They were everywhere, dislocating the granite paving slabs as they snaked upwards with rough, sinuous limbs, eager for the sun, all set to trip up the careless. Those ones over there were particularly awful-looking, all gnarled and twisted into corkscrews...

'You couldn't wait, could you?'

Vittie's blood turned ice cold at the stranger's voice. She stifled a scream as the twisted roots shuffled towards her, a millimetre at a time. Fear and revulsion coursed through her as they came closer, for these were no roots, they were toenails; dirty-yellow corkscrewy toenails that had never stopped growing even after...

'I...I...waited and waited, b...b...but no one...'

'LOOK at me when you speak to me, girl!'

Don't, Vittie! Don't look at him! You know what happens when you look into a zombie's face!

But a force stronger than her will was tilting her face up, up, up... Vittie looked at the stranger's face, into the hollows where the eyeballs should have been, at the shining mane of thick, long black hair that billowed like a live thing around the grinning skull.

As the pale, skeletal hands, tipped with never-ending yellow fingernails, reached for her, Vittie began to scream.

Makes for a great horror story, huh? But that's just what it is: a story. Hair and fingernails—and toenails!—simply do not grow after you're dead.

DO ALL OUR CELLS DIE THE MOMENT WE DIE?

What does 'to die' really mean when we talk about human beings? Usually, it means 'the state when the heart stops beating for more than a few minutes'. And what is a heartbeat, really? It is the opening and the closing of your heart's valves as it pumps oxygen-rich blood around your body.

Every cell of your body needs a continuous supply of oxygen to survive, to work, and to produce new cells to replace old, dead ones. This is because all the energy to keep your cells running smoothly comes from the burning of glucose, which happens in the presence of oxygen. Cut off the oxygen supply to your cells, and most will be dead—forever—in less than ten minutes.

The nerve cells—all part of the brain—are the first to go, within three to seven minutes after oxygen supply is cut off to the brain. The kidney, liver and the heart itself can survive for as long as thirty minutes and if they are taken out of the body within that time, they can be preserved on ice for a few more hours. That's the reason why heart, liver and kidney transplants are possible. Skin cells can live much longer: skin can be taken off a dead person up to twelve hours after his or her death, and grafted on to another person!

WHAT ABOUT NAIL AND HAIR CELLS?

Well, in the first place, nail and hair cells—at least the cells of your *visible* nails and hair—are made up of a fibrous protein called keratin, and composed of cells that are already dead. These cells have no blood, no muscles, and no nerves. This is why getting a haircut or clipping your nails is painless and bloodless.

How does something composed of dead cells *grow*, though? Good question. Let's talk hair first. Each strand of hair grows out of a hair follicle inside our skin. At the base of each follicle is the papilla—the hair 'bud'—which is very much alive and well-supplied with blood and oxygen. Imagine it as root of the plant that is your hair. It is at the papilla that all the hair growth happens. As new cells are made here, they push up the older ones, and your hair 'grows'. The moment the new cells emerge out of your body, they die.

A similar thing happens with nails. There's a layer of tissue

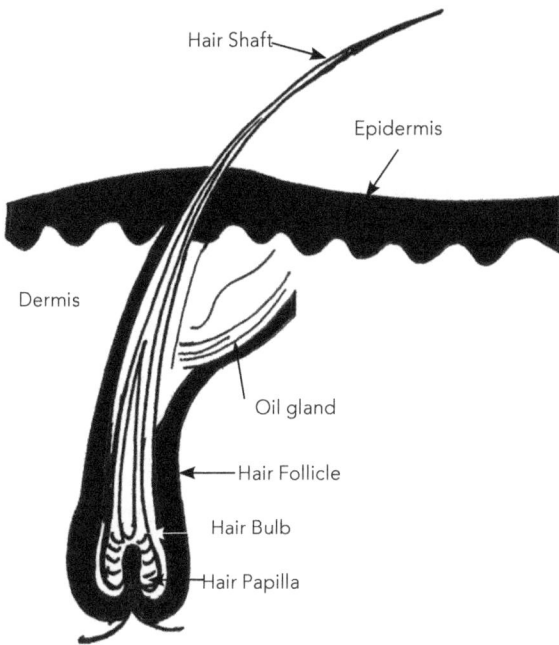

Portrait of a hair follicle

below the base of each fingernail or toenail called the germinal matrix, which is where all new cells are born. As in the case of hair, the germinal matrix is also well supplied with blood and oxygen, otherwise it would not be able to produce new cells. The new cells push the older ones up and out, making it appear to us that nail growth is actually happening at the tips of our nails instead of at its base.

When we die, oxygen supply is cut off to both the papillae of all our hair and the germinal matrix below all our nails, making it impossible for them to burn glucose to release energy to help them function as they should. *Which, in turn, makes it impossible for our hair and nails to continue growing after we die.*

How did this 'scientifically-proven' myth become so popular, though? For a very good reason, actually. When we die, our skin loses water and *shrinks*, pulling back from our nails, creating the *impression* that they have gotten longer. The skin on our face also pulls back, making our hair—particularly the stubble on men's cheeks and chins—look more prominent and visible.

So, yeah, it's good material for a hair-raising story, but good old science has put the last nail in that particular coffin.

YOUR TONGUE HAS A 'TASTE MAP'

Every school science text book has a diagram of the tongue's taste map, with different areas of the tongue marked off and labelled. According to this map, we taste sweetness more at the tips of our tongues, saltiness along the edges, sourness on the sides, and bitterness way at the back. But guess what? This taste map of the tongue, which students all over the world have memorized for a hundred years, is a complete myth!

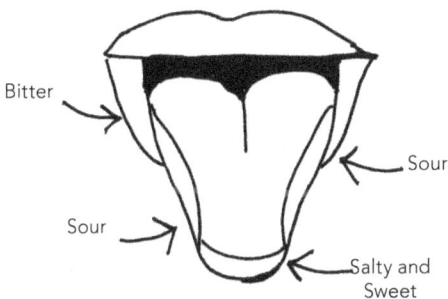

A question of taste

HOW DO WE TASTE?

How do we know if we are eating yummy chocolate or yucky old karela ? How do we know the instant we put something in our mouths whether it is fresh or stale? Why do we love junk food so much? It all has to do with the hundreds of tiny sensitive spheres, called taste buds, which carpet our tongues and help us enjoy (or absolutely detest) what we eat and drink.

The tongue is not a smooth canvas of taste buds, though. Its surface is covered with thousands of papillae—the little bumps that give the tongue its rough texture. Most of these papillae contain taste buds, and there are taste buds in between the papillae as well—in short, many, many taste buds.

Now, each taste bud is made up of taste receptor cells, clustered around a tiny central hole opening on to the surface of the tongue. Each taste-receptor cell is specialized, and detects one particular basic taste only. A miniscule 'sensor hair' snakes out of each cell through the hole of the taste bud, where it waits, eager and alert, for the next taste to pass through.

When it does, the taste receptor cells sense it, and quickly pass the information on to the bundle of nerve cells at the bottom of each taste bud, which instantly relay it to the brain for analysis and feedback. If the brain recognizes the taste as a good one, you will begin to enjoy your meal, if it doesn't, you will wish you were eating something else.

Most of us know of the four basic tastes: sweet, sour, bitter, and salty. The other tastes—pungent (spicy), aromatic, astringent, metallic, and many more—are believed to be unique combinations of the four basic tastes. More and more scientists and researchers, however, now agree there is a fifth basic taste called 'Umami', which is the taste of rich and meaty protein flavours. There is also a debate on as to whether we have a sixth basic taste receptor for fat.

There is another element in how we taste. A lot of what we imagine we are 'tasting' is a result of what happens not just via our taste buds, *but via our noses*! Yes, our pleasure in certain foods—coffee, chocolate and tandoori chicken, for instance, or foods that have butter, ghee, cinnamon or cardamom in them—comes as much from their *smell* as from their taste. That's why most food doesn't appeal as much as it usually does when we have a cold and our noses are blocked!

Here's another cool fact: some people taste better than others! (Oh, before you go off to test this theory by cutting off a piece of your friend's ear and bar-be-cueing it, here's a clarification: the previous sentence isn't meant in a cannibalistic way, but in the sense that some people's tongues are far more sensitive to basic tastes than others'.) How come? They just have more taste buds per square centimetre of tongue! Supertasters—the guys who are employed by the food industry and paid tons of money for their talent—have an average of 425 per sq cm, medium tasters have about 185, and non-tasters (that doesn't mean they can't taste anything, it just means that they are less sensitive to minor changes in taste than others) have a mere 96. (Are YOU a supertaster? Find out in the box on page 82.)

WHY DO SOME FOODS APPEAL MORE THAN OTHERS?

Why do we love sweet things, and fatty things, and salty things so much? Because of evolution! Thousands of years ago, before agriculture began, all human beings were hunter-gatherers who had to forage for their food like every other animal. They could not be choosy about what they ate—they had to eat what they found, and they could rarely predict what, or when, they would be eating next.

So when they did come across something sweet—which meant that it was loaded with sugars and carbohydrates, both essential for energy—they would totally load up on it, and their bodies would store the extra energy away for the future. The same logic applied to fat—a gram of fat provides us with 9 calories of energy, which is more than double the energy a gram of carbohydrate or protein provides! No wonder our ancestors fell on fatty foods with such glad 'Ugga! Ugga!'s of delight whenever and wherever they found it.

It is evolution that makes us dislike bitter and sour things too. To our foraging ancestors, a bitter taste meant that the food was likely to be poisonous, and sour meant that the food was either unripe or spoilt. Salty things appealed because eating them would replenish the salts lost through sweat—after all, they did walk miles and miles each day hunting and gathering their food.

Today, of course, we can decide exactly what we are going to eat next, and when, but our brains still send out the same signal when we see or taste something sweet or fatty or salty—GORGE! And we do.

ARE YOU A SUPERTASTER?

YOU MIGHT BE! AND YOUR CHANCES ARE WAY HIGHER IF YOU SATISFY THE FOLLOWING CONDITIONS:

* YOU ARE FEMALE. (TESTS HAVE SHOWN THAT 35% OF WOMEN ARE SUPERTASTERS, AS AGAINST 15% OF MEN.)
* YOU ARE FROM ASIA, AFRICA OR SOUTH AMERICA. (MANY MORE SUPERTASTERS COME FROM THESE CONTINENTS THAN FROM THE OTHERS. DON'T KNOW ABOUT THE OTHERS, BUT AS FAR AS INDIANS ARE CONCERNED, THE HEIGHTENED SENSITIVITY TO TASTES MUST BE FROM ALL THE DIFFERENT SPICES AND WONDERFUL FLAVOURS THAT ARE SUCH A BIG PART OF OUR FOOD.)
* YOU DON'T PARTICULARLY LIKE CABBAGE, KARELA, COFFEE, GREEN TEA AND SOY MILK. (ACTUALLY, MOST CHILDREN DON'T LIKE THESE FOODS. SCIENTISTS BELIEVE THIS IS BECAUSE CHILDREN CAN TASTE FLAVOURS MORE ACUTELY—THAT'S ALSO WHY THEY ARE SO OFTEN FUSSY ABOUT THEIR FOOD. THEN THEY GROW UP AND START DRINKING COFFEE BY THE BUCKETFUL, AND LOSE ALL THAT WONDERFUL TASTE SENSITIVITY.)
* YOU DON'T LIKE CARBONATED DRINKS, CANDY, OR FRENCH FRIES VERY MUCH EITHER. (A-HA! NOT SO MANY OF YOU NODDING SO VIGOROUSLY NOW, ARE YOU? BUT SUPERTASTERS FEEL FLAVOURS SO STRONGLY THAT THEY FIND SALTY THINGS TOO SALTY, SWEET THINGS TOO SWEET, AND BITTER THINGS TOO BITTER, SO THEY NORMALLY STAY AWAY FROM THEM. AS A BONUS, THEY STAY REALLY HEALTHY!)
* YOUR DREAM IS TO WIN MASTERCHEF JUNIOR AND/OR TO RUN YOUR

SO WE DON'T TASTE CERTAIN TASTES ON CERTAIN PARTS OF OUR TONGUES?

Apparently not. In fact, research conducted as far back as 1974 proved quite conclusively that EVERY taste bud has taste-receptor cells for EVERY basic taste, in clusters of 50-100 cells per taste. There could be variations in sensitivity for certain tastes across the tongue, but those variations are minor, and different for each individual.

It is surprising that we still know so little about the simple mechanism of tasting, when we know so much more about the more complex mechanisms of seeing and hearing. But it is even more surprising that school textbooks still carry a diagram of the tongue's taste map, forty years after it was proven to be nothing but a tasteless myth.

SECTION III

10 MIND-NUMBING MYSTERIES THAT AREN'T REALLY MYSTERIOUS AT ALL

HOW ARE WE SMARTER THAN SPERM WHALES, EVEN THOUGH OUR BRAINS ARE WAY SMALLER THAN THEIRS?

Okay. There are a couple of things we need to debate right at the beginning. Things like: What exactly does 'smart' mean? Aren't there tons of ways in which animals are 'smarter' than us? Dogs have a much better sense of smell, eagles have far better eyesight, owls have such keen hearing they would put ours to shame. Knowing all this, how do we humans still have the gall to think we're the 'smartest' of all the earth's creatures?

Let's tackle the first question first. Let's assume 'smart' is the same as 'intelligent'. According to the dictionary, 'intelligence' is 'the ability to acquire and apply knowledge and skills'. Wikipedia says intelligence includes stuff like:

- abstract thought ('What would happen if the sun disappeared?');
- understanding ('That's not going to happen anytime soon');
- self-awareness ('And when the sun does disappear, I won't be around, so there's no need to worry about it');
- communication ('Hey, I am going to post a fake news item on Google+ that the sun is going to disappear in ten days, and scare the pants off everyone! LOL!');

- reasoning ('Ahhh, no point, today is April 1 and they'll all figure out they're being pranked! ☹');
- learning ('I'll still do it, but I'll do it after a couple of days');
- remembering things ('It's so going to work! Just like everyone was so psyched about the end of the world in December 2012!');
- planning ('Oh, but I'm going away on vacation day after tomorrow, so how am I going to put it on g+?');
- problem solving ('I'll have to con Mom into letting me use her smartphone');
- having 'emotional knowledge' ('Mom's always in a good mood when we're on holiday so getting her phone will be a piece of cake. Hurray!')

If we accept these definitions of 'intelligence', the second question is not valid anymore. Because having a better sense of smell, or vision, or hearing, does not make you 'intelligent'. Being able to spot a rat from 15,000 feet up in the air is great, but knowing how to build a rat trap so that you can stop hunting for each meal and free up time for watching TV is something only humans have figured out how to do. (Of course most of us don't eat rats, but you know what we mean, don't you?)

As for the last question, you can see for yourself! Look how easily we have demonstrated over the last page that humans are indeed more intelligent than animals using a definition of intelligence that we humans ourselves came up with! We are really, really good at this kind of stuff—at proving things that make us feel good about ourselves. That's all there is to it!

BUT SERIOUSLY, HOW ARE WE ABLE TO ACHIEVE SUCH A LOT WITH SUCH A SMALL BRAIN?

Ah. Now we come to the real question. Does the size of one's brain really matter? In other words, does having a bigger brain mean you are smarter? According to scientists and researchers, yes and no. Apparently, the ACTUAL size of your brain, whether it is 1.5 kg (the weight of an average human brain) or 9 kg (the weight of an average sperm whale brain) is not what is important. What is important is how heavy your brain is *in comparison with your body*!

If you compare an average human's brain weight (1.5 kg) to her body weight (60 kg), you find that her body is about 40 times the weight of her brain. Do the same for a sperm whale (9 kg brain to 40,000 kg body), and you realize that the whale's body is 4,444 times heavier than its brain!

Obviously, that huge whale brain, even though it is 6 times bigger than a human brain, is likely to be fully occupied at all times just figuring out what the messages coming to it from the whale's faraway tail mean, and what action the whale should take in response. If the message is 'Just felt a harpoon whiz by!', for instance, the whale brain will have to send messages to every corner of its 60-foot-long body, all of them yelling, 'Zoom out of range! *Now!*'

As you can imagine, the whale's brain would be too exhausted after that to come up with a new 'Zombies Vs Aliens' app or a cool way to download music illegally. The human brain, on the other hand, having only a 6 foot long body's messages to worry about, has enough and more time to do stuff like that.

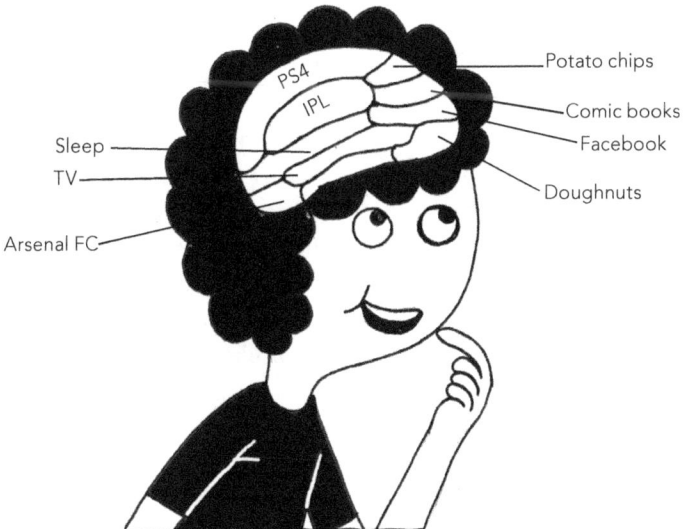

Brain to body weight ratio in different animals

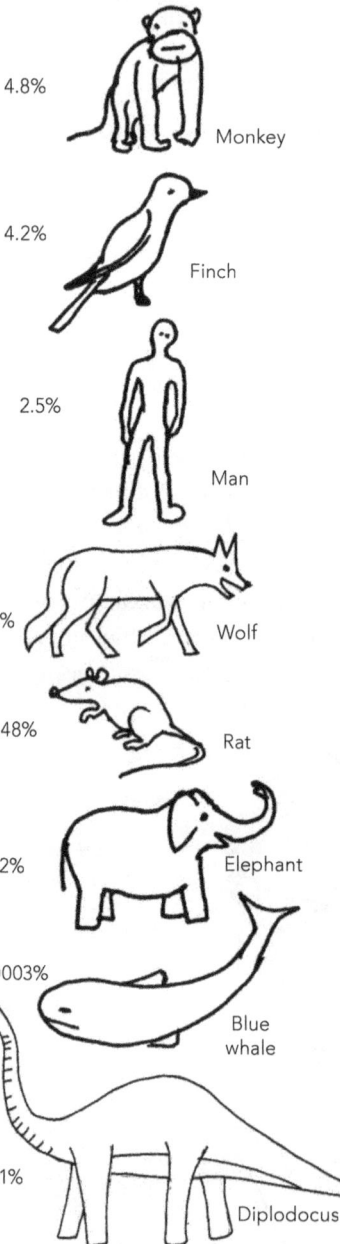

4.8% — Monkey

4.2% — Finch

2.5% — Man

0.85% — Wolf

0.48% — Rat

0.2% — Elephant

0.0003% — Blue whale

0.0001% — Diplodocus

However, some researchers did not agree with this kind of measurement. If this were the accurate way to measure brain power, they said reasonably, rats would be as smart as humans, since their bodies were ALSO about 40 times bigger than their brains, and small birds would be MUCH smarter than us (since their bodies are only about 12 times heavier than their brains). But that, of course, is not true, at least from what we observe and understand of animal behaviour.

So these researchers went away and puzzled over this for many years, and finally came up with another way to measure brain power, called the 'Encephalization Quotient', which is as difficult to explain as it is to pronounce. All you need to know about it is that it is a formula to calculate intelligence in mammals, which involves comparing brain sizes of animals of similar body sizes. When they put in brain sizes and body sizes of various mammals into THIS formula and calculated the results, voila! Humans came out as THE MOST INTELLIGENT MAMMALS!

Dolphins (bottlenose dolphins and orcas) came next on the list, followed by apes (chimpanzees), monkeys (our good old rhesus monkeys), elephants, dogs, squirrels and cats. This is something we all know to be true from observing these animals– all of them are 'intelligent'; they have 'the ability to acquire and apply knowledge and skills'. Which sort of proved that this formula was a good way to calculate IQ.

BUT HOW IS THERE SUCH A HUGE GAP BETWEEN HUMAN AND DOLPHIN INTELLIGENCE IF DOLPHINS ARE THE SECOND MOST INTELLIGENT?

Well, for one thing, because our brains have so many neurons. Neurons are the building blocks of our nervous system (the brain, the spinal cord and our nerves–all of which are connected either to the brain or to the spinal cord or both–form our body's nervous system). The tree-like branches of neurons connect with other neurons, forming the complex machine called the brain. All animal brains have neurons, but none have AS MANY NEURONS as ours–a staggering 86-100 billion of them–all passing millions of messages continuously between themselves, and between the brain and other parts of the body!

But how do so many neurons fit in our small brains? Because of all the folds! Our brain is much more folded and wrinkled than that of other animals, and folds and wrinkles means more surface area for neurons to occupy. More neurons mean more routes available for thinking many thoughts, or more complex thoughts;

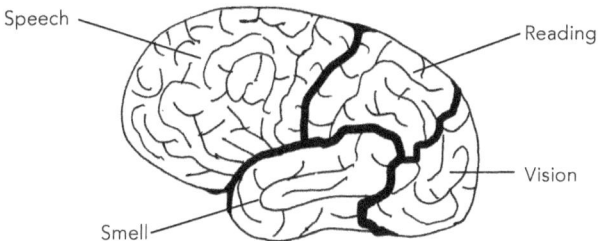

Speech — Reading — Vision — Smell

and doing more complex actions too (Bharatanayam, driving a car, tennis)!

But it isn't just the number of neurons we have that makes us smarter—the really unique thing about the human brain is the size of our cerebral cortex. The cerebral cortex is a 3 mm thick web of brain cells that 'wraps' around most of our brain, and it is this wrapping that is mainly responsible for memory, attention, awareness of surroundings, thought, language, consciousness—in short, all the things that make human beings human.

You see, every animal's brain has the part which controls breathing, blood circulation, digestion, excretion etc., and the part that responds to signals from the environment around it. ('It's hot!' 'It's raining!' 'That looks dangerous!') BUT no other animal has as big or as wrinkled or as developed a cerebral cortex as we do.

And THAT's why, as far as we know, humans are more 'intelligent' than other animals.

WHY IS IT THAT MY THROAT INFECTION GOES AWAY WHEN I TAKE ANTIBIOTICS, BUT MY COLD DOESN'T?

Good question. In fact, while serious stuff like pneumonia, food poisoning and scarlet fever vanish without a trace after a round of antibiotics, *nothing* seems to ever work on a cold.

To understand why a cold is so resistant to medication, we need to understand the difference between a bacterium and a virus. Huh, you say, what do bacteria and viruses have to do with anything? Everything, as it turns out!

BADASS BACTERIA VS VILE VIRUSES

First of all, both bacteria and viruses are E-V-I-L.

Nope, we're just kidding, that's not strictly true. While there are a lot of bacteria and viruses that can hurt us, we have plenty of bacteria—and one virus—to thank for a bunch of things.

For instance, the millions and millions of bacteria that live in our digestive system—in our mouths, oesophaguses (the tube that takes your food down to the stomach), stomachs and intestines—not only help us digest our food but are so good at speedily populating our gut that there is no room for bad bacteria to move in. Oh, and these same bacteria are also responsible for making us fart (we fart because of the gas the bacteria in our guts produce after gorging on OUR food!)

Outside of our bodies, bacteria help turn milk into curd and cheese, help clean up the environment by eating their way through oil spills and dead matter (yeah, these guys' diets are pretty gross), and even produce natural gas deep inside the earth for us to use as fuel.

What *are* bacteria, though? Bacteria are organisms that are so tiny you can only see them under a microscope. There are thousands of kinds, but each of them is only made up of one solitary cell. (To put that in perspective: your little toe is made up of at least a couple of billion cells.) Their size doesn't stop them from doing everything you do, though—they eat, turn their food into the energy they need, grow, and produce other bacteria just like themselves.

Unlike the not-so-badass-after-all bacteria, vile viruses are nearly all evil. They are even smaller than bacteria, they are everywhere, and they cause diseases in just about everyone and everything—plants, animals, even bacteria! And these days, they even infect computers! (Haha, not really. Computer viruses can be a pain, but they are not the kind of viruses we are talking about here.)

The only virus that is sort of good for us is the cowpox virus. Well, it isn't exactly 'good', but it did help British doctor Edward Jenner discover a vaccine for one of the world's deadliest diseases ever—smallpox.

Now, what exactly is a virus? And how different is it from a bacterium? Well, if you thought being one-celled was a bit of a handicap, viruses are at even more of a disadvantage—they aren't even that! They are just a strand of DNA in a protein jacket. (DNA, as we discussed before while talking about dinosaurs, is present in every single live cell in the world, and it contains instructions to help living things do what they do—convert the food they eat into energy to grow and reproduce.)

DO BACTERIA AND VIRUSES MAKE US ILL IN THE SAME WAY?

Not at all.

Once bad bacteria get past our body's defences and into our bloodstream, they float around between our cells, multiplying rapidly. Then they turn on us, either eating up our healthy cells or polluting them with some fairly deadly poisons that kill our cells or prevent them from doing their jobs. Of course our body's 'immune system'–our crack team of germ-fighting cells–soon swings into action, but by this time, the bacteria are too many for them to combat. In fact, the pain that you feel when you have a bacterial infection–throat ache, stomach ache, pain around an open wound as it heals–is more because of your immune system's reaction to the bacteria than the bacteria themselves.

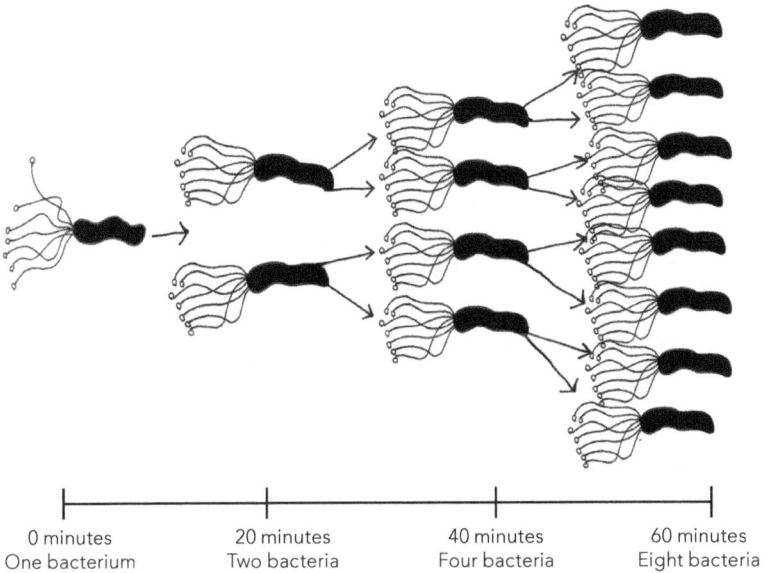

| 0 minutes | 20 minutes | 40 minutes | 60 minutes |
| One bacterium | Two bacteria | Four bacteria | Eight bacteria |

Speed demons: How one bacterium becomes a billion (okay, eight)

A virus operates very differently. Because viruses aren't even whole cells, they can't eat, grow or reproduce by themselves. Outside a living cell, they are 'dormant', or asleep. But because they contain the instructions to do everything that a living cell does, all they need to do is grab any living cell with their specially designed prongs, slink in, and fool the cell into thinking that this new strand of DNA floating around in it is also its own. Once that happens, the cell simply starts following the virus DNA's recipes along with its own, especially the virus DNA's powerful 'reproduction recipe'.

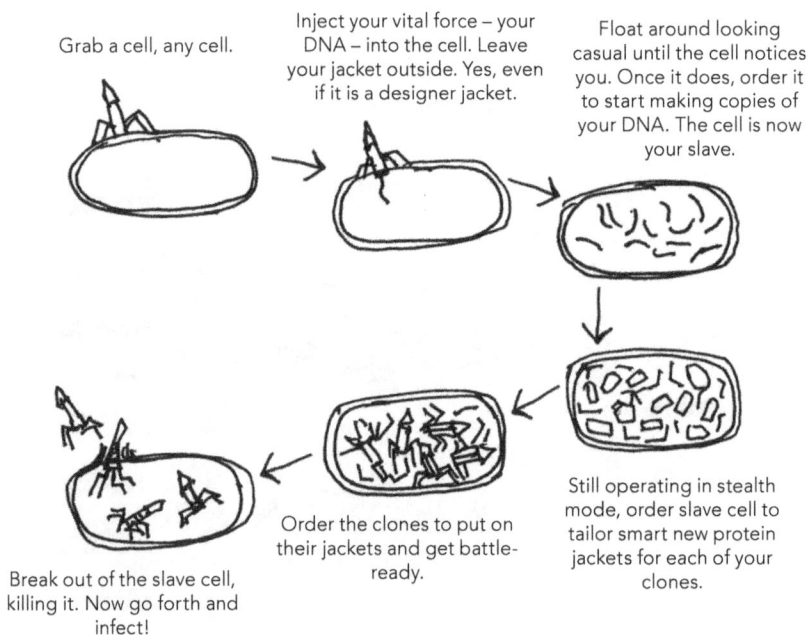

Grab a cell, any cell.

Inject your vital force – your DNA – into the cell. Leave your jacket outside. Yes, even if it is a designer jacket.

Float around looking casual until the cell notices you. Once it does, order it to start making copies of your DNA. The cell is now your slave.

Still operating in stealth mode, order slave cell to tailor smart new protein jackets for each of your clones.

Order the clones to put on their jackets and get battle-ready.

Break out of the slave cell, killing it. Now go forth and infect!

How to go viral: A step-by-step guide
(Top secret: For virus eyes only)

Before you know it, the cell has made so many new viruses that it explodes. Fleets of bad viruses enter your bloodstream, and the process repeats. Each new virus sinks its prongs into a healthy cell, and the hostile takeover begins again.

Once again, your body's immune system launches an attack. Most times, the immune system can control the virus by itself, which is why most of us are healthy most of the time. But sometimes, your immune system needs some help from you.

WHAT DOES ALL THIS HAVE TO DO WITH ANTIBIOTICS?

Ah yes. We are coming to that now. Antibiotics are a special kind of drug designed to help your body combat infections, and they are pretty powerful. Different antibiotics work in different ways to control infection, but here's the thing–*they all work only on bacteria!*

None of them can do a thing about viruses, because viruses aren't even alive. Plus, the viruses are already in your cells, so killing them would mean killing off your own healthy cells too! See how devious viruses are?

And THAT'S why your throat infection (which is caused by bacteria) disappears so quickly after a dose of antibiotics, and why your common cold (which is caused by viruses) is so completely unaffected by them.

Don't worry too much about it, though. A new class of drug called antivirals have recently been developed which work against specific viruses. You can also be protected against many deadly viral diseases–including small pox, chicken pox, tetanus, measles, mumps, rabies, influenza and more–by taking the appropriate vaccine.

As for your cold, haven't you heard the old piece of wisdom– 'A cold is cured in seven days with medication and in a week without'? So just cover up nice and warm, and curl up with a good book and a thermos of hot soup. Sounds good, hunh? Acchhoo!

WHO MOVED MY POX?

WAY BACK IN THE EIGHTEENTH CENTURY, SMALLPOX (CAUSED BY THE DEADLY VIRUS TWINS VARIOLA MAJOR AND VARIOLA MINOR) WAS A KILLER DISEASE, KILLING OVER HALF THE PEOPLE AND ALMOST EVERY CHILD WHO CAUGHT IT. DOCTORS ALL OVER THE WORLD WERE DESPERATELY LOOKING FOR A CURE, OR AT LEAST A PREVENTIVE, FOR THE TERRIBLE DISEASE.

ONE OF THEM WAS A CLEVER BRITISH DOCTOR CALLED EDWARD JENNER, WHO NOTICED THAT MILKMAIDS NEVER SEEMED TO CATCH SMALLPOX. FURTHER INVESTIGATION REVEALED THAT ALL OF THOSE MILKMAIDS HAD AT SOME TIME IN THEIR LIVES HAD COWPOX (A DISEASE CAUSED BY THE VIRUS VACCINIA, VERY SIMILAR TO BUT FAR LESS DANGEROUS THAN THE VARIOLAS), WHICH THEY HAD CAUGHT FROM THEIR COWS.

JENNER WONDERED IF GETTING COWPOX SOMEHOW PREVENTED PEOPLE FROM GETTING SMALLPOX. HE BEGAN EXPERIMENTING ON MANY HEALTHY PEOPLE DURING A SMALLPOX EPIDEMIC, FORCIBLY GIVING THEM COWPOX SO THAT THEY WOULDN'T GET SMALLPOX.

ONE OF THE PEOPLE HE EXPERIMENTED ON WAS EIGHT-YEAR-OLD JAMES PHIPPS. FILLING A SYRINGE WITH FLUID FROM A COWPOX BLISTER ON A MILKMAID'S ARM, THE GOOD DOCTOR (WHO WOULD HAVE BEEN THROWN INTO JAIL IF HE HAD TRIED ANYTHING LIKE THIS TODAY) INJECTED JAMES WITH IT. THE BOY CAME DOWN WITH A MILD FEVER FOR A COUPLE OF DAYS, BUT HE NEVER CAUGHT COWPOX OR SMALLPOX, *EVEN WHEN HE WAS INJECTED WITH THE SMALLPOX VIRUS A COUPLE OF WEEKS LATER!*

WHEN HE HAD BEEN INJECTED WITH THE PUS, PHIPPS'S DISEASE-FIGHTING CELLS HAD GONE TO WAR AGAINST THE WEAK VACCINIA, AND LEARNT HOW TO DESTROY

THEM SUCCESSFULLY. WHEN VARIOLA CAME ALONG TWO WEEKS LATER, IT LOOKED SO SIMILAR TO VACCINIA THAT PHIPPS' DISEASE-FIGHTING CELLS INSTANTLY REMEMBERED WHAT THEY HAD DONE THE LAST TIME AND PROCEEDED TO DESTROY THE VARIOLAS TOO. NEVER AGAIN WOULD THE VARIOLAS BE ABLE TO INFECT PHIPPS.

AND THAT'S THE HEROIC STORY OF THE ONLY 'GOOD' VIRUS WE KNOW—VACCINIA—WHICH NOT ONLY GAVE US THE WORD VACCINE (YOU CAN GUESS WHY IT'S CALLED THAT, CAN'T YOU?) BUT HELPED DR JENNER ERADICATE SMALLPOX FROM THE FACE OF THE EARTH.

Still not sure what a vaccine is? Here's the short answer. When you get 'vaccinated' against a disease, say cholera, the doctor is basically forcibly injecting germs that cause cholera into your bloodstream. That's not as bizarre as it sounds, because the whole exercise is a 'trial run' for your germ-fighting cells. As soon as they spot the intruders, your germ-fighting cells go to war, and they win easily—because the cholera germs in the vaccine are very weak ones. What is the point of this? The point is that now your body's immune system has learnt how to fight these particular germs. So when the strong cholera germs attack you in the future, your body is much better prepared to recognize and defeat them.

HOW COME MY FINGERS AND TOES GET ALL WRINKLY WHEN I STAY TOO LONG IN THE POOL, BUT NOT MY FACE?

A real mystery that, don't you think? In fact, scientists and researchers are still coming up with new theories on why our fingertips turn into raisins when they've been in water for a while, because no one is quite certain yet. And guess what—most other animals don't have this 'post-soak-raisiny-fingertip syndrome' at all! So what exactly makes our fingertips wrinkle, and is that a good or bad thing?

SKIN IS IN

Let's begin with what everyone's favourite theory about fingertip wrinkling is. To understand it, you must first, erm, get under your skin.

You probably already know this, but the largest human organ is...no, not your intestines or your lungs or your kidneys, but your skin! If you think about it, your skin is pretty cool. It envelops every part of you like a perfectly-tailored, snug-fitting (well, at least until you get all ancient and wrinkly all over), 'breathable', completely waterproof, all-weather suit of armour that grows along with you!

'Breathable', because while it doesn't let the air get in, it certainly lets the sweat out through millions of tiny pores, cooling your body in the process. Waterproof, because of a lubricating oil called sebum that it manufactures and squeezes out on to its surface at regular intervals, creating a layer of biological cling wrap (if it wasn't for sebum, you'd be swelling up like a sponge every time you jumped in a pool and drying out like a papad when you were out in the sun too long). The skin's also a suit of armour, because it doesn't let ANYTHING harmful get past it—not germs, not dirt, not pollutants.

A TRIPLE-DECKER SANDWICH

Now that we have established that skin is a rockstar, let's talk about its structure a little. Our skin is made up of three layers—the top layer, the one that we see, is the epidermis.

The epidermis is really just several wafer-thin sheets of skin cells and melanocytes (the cells that give our skin its colour: rich brown Indian skin has far more melanocytes than pale western skin for a reason. If we didn't have as many as we do, our skins would burn in the harsh Indian sun). It is the epidermis that has the pores through which your hair grows out, and your sweat and sebum ooze. The top layer of the epidermis is just dead cells that keep falling off through the day (get ready to get grossed out—a large part of the dust in your house is actually *dead skin cells*). This is a continuous process—as new cells are born inside your skin, the old ones get pushed to the top, die and flake off.

Just below the epidermis is the dermis. In the dermis are the blood vessels that carry blood to and from the skin; the nerves that help us feel things like temperature changes and are responsible for one of our five senses—touch; the roots of our hair (and we're not just talking about the stuff on your head—all mammals have hair all over their bodies, except on their palms and on the soles of their feet); the oil glands that secrete sebum; and of course, the sweat glands.

Attached to the dermis and below it is the hypodermis, which is made up mostly of fatty tissue. Just like the thick layer of blubber below a blue whale's skin keeps it warm in the freezing Arctic seas, the hypodermis of our skin is our cushion and insulator. The one big difference: a single blue whale has about 50,000 kg of blubber! While we have...well, let's just stop right there and not embarrass ourselves.

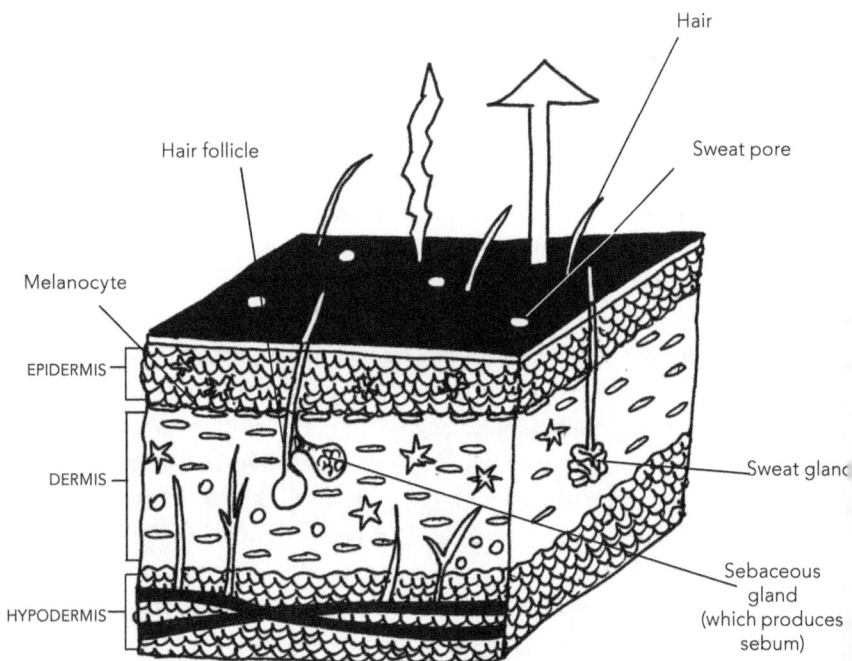

Skin: The inside story

CAN WE GET TO THE RAISINY FINGERTIPS ALREADY?

Sure. So here's the popular theory on fingertip wrinkling. When we soak in water for a long time, the sebum that makes our skin waterproof washes off a little. The dead cells on the top layer of the epidermis, which are mainly made up of a protein called keratin (the same stuff that's in our nails and hair), begin to absorb water and swell up. But this layer is still attached tightly to the layer of living keratin cells (which do not absorb water) below. Wrinkling gives the temporarily larger top layer somewhere to go while it is still attached to the lower layer! Simple!

But how are only the fingertips and toes affected then? How is it that the rest of our skin doesn't wrinkle too? Well, since we use our palms and feet so much, the top layer of skin there is thicker than skin elsewhere. That means these places have more dead keratin cells that can absorb water!

It's pretty convincing as a theory, and most people still swear by it. But then doctors began to notice something—if the nerves in the fingertips were affected or destroyed for some reason, *the fingertips did not wrinkle!* Even after they were soaked for hours in water! That's when scientists began to suspect that it wasn't the skin itself, but the *nervous system* that was making our fingertips wrinkle.

Some scientists now say that it isn't because the top layer of skin *swells*, but because the lower layers *shrink*, that wrinkles happen. When the body has been in water for a long time, it begins to get cold. One of the nervous system's ways to help the body conserve heat is to make the arteries (the tubes that carry blood from the heart to different parts of the body) contract, so that less blood reaches the surface of the skin and gives up its heat to the atmosphere. When the arteries contract, they pull the surrounding cells in, making those layers of skin shrink too. The top un-shrunk layer (which doesn't shrink because it's made up of dead cells) HAS to wrinkle to stay the same size as the lower layer.

RAISINY FINGERTIPS ARE COOL, BUT NOTHING MORE. OR ARE THEY?

Other animals' fingertips don't wrinkle—except certain primates like macaques—so in that sense our wrinkly fingertips set us apart and make us special. But there's probably more to it than that. Some scientists who study evolution to understand why human bodies are the way they are today think that making fingertips wrinkly was probably nature's way of helping our ancestors get a better grip on slippery things in water, like fish, or wet vegetation, when they went foraging for food, just like a car tyre's 'treads' help it to get a better grip on the surface of a wet road!

Which theory do YOU think is the more likely one? If you ticked 'None of the above', wonderful. Now you can go off and think about a new theory, all your own. Like they say, there's more than one way to 'skin' a cat.

WHY IS IT SO COLD IN JANUARY, EVEN THOUGH THE EARTH IS CLOSEST TO THE SUN THEN?

First, another question. How many of you actually knew that the earth is closest to the sun in January? No fibbing, mind! Not many hands going up now, are there? But the astounding truth is that the earth is closest to the sun around 3 January every year, and furthest away–hold your breath–in sweltering July! How come? To understand the answer to this, we should first find the answer to another question:

WHAT ACTUALLY CAUSES THE SEASONS?

If you have always believed, like most people, that we have summer when the earth is closer to the sun and winter when it is further away, well, you've got it ALL wrong. The earth's distance from the sun does have a minor effect on the temperatures here on earth, but the really MAJOR effect–the thing that actually causes summer and winter to happen–is the tilt of the earth's axis.

If the earth was not tilted at all (notice how globes also are always tilted; the north pole is never facing straight up) the whole earth would have had similar temperatures through the year, with the regions around the equator–on which the sun's rays would fall directly–being the warmest and the regions closer to the poles—on which the sun's rays would fall obliquely (nice word, right? It means slantingly, except slantingly is not a word.) being the coolest.

Which would have been okay, except that we would miss all the seasonal excitement like the kulfi in summer and hot pakoras in winter and people would have to constantly travel from one place to another to experience a change of weather, which, after a point, would be quite tiring.

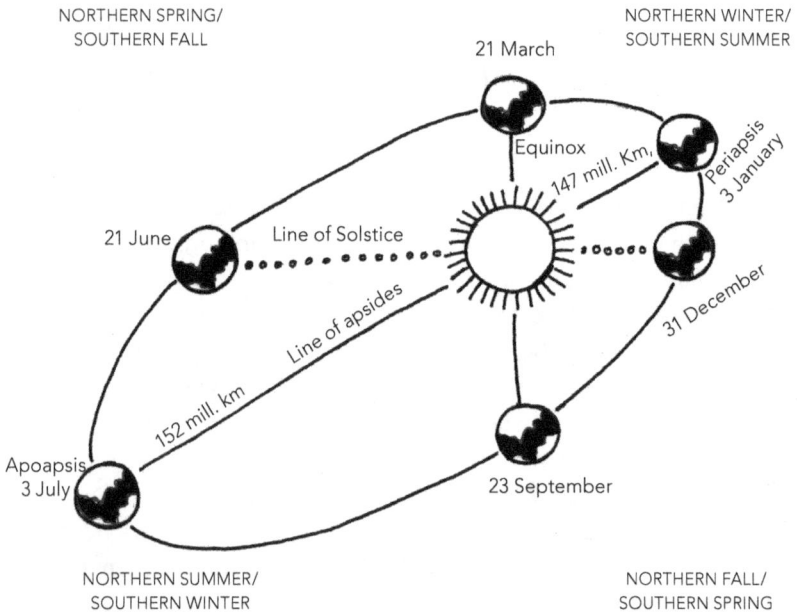

NORTHERN SPRING/
SOUTHERN FALL

21 March

NORTHERN WINTER/
SOUTHERN SUMMER

Equinox

147 mill. Km,

Periapsis
3 January

21 June

Line of Solstice

Line of apsides

31 December

152 mill. km

Apoapsis
3 July

23 September

NORTHERN SUMMER/
SOUTHERN WINTER

NORTHERN FALL/
SOUTHERN SPRING

Sun: Near yet so far away

Luckily, though, the earth's axis has a pretty significant tilt—23.5 degrees—away from the straight-up. That means the northern hemisphere, where India is, is tilted *towards* the sun for some part of the year and *away* from the sun for another part. When our hemisphere is tilted towards the sun, the sun falls directly—and for more hours each day–on our part of the world, and we have summer. When we are tilted away from the sun, the sun rays fall obliquely–and for fewer hours–on our part of the world, and we have winter.

Obviously, when our hemisphere is tilted towards the sun, the earth's other hemisphere is tilted away, and vice versa. So down there in the southern hemisphere (in places like Australia and South Africa), they have the seasons all wrong (well, according to us northerners anyway). They have summer in December and winter in June!

The thing is, the closer you live to the Equator, where the sun's rays more or less fall directly through the year, the less variation there is in the seasons. In south India, or Singapore, or Dubai, all places closer to the Equator, for instance, there isn't much difference between summer temperatures and winter temperatures. The tilt of the earth doesn't really affect these places much. But if you live up in the temperate zones of the earth, where the sun's light falls obliquely for most of the year, things could get mighty chilly around winter.

There are also a bunch of other things that determine why one place is hotter or colder than another, even when the two places are at the same distance from the Equator. Things like how high the place is above sea level (Bangalore and Chennai are exactly the same distance from the equator, but Bangalore is cooler because it is higher); how close it is to the sea (Delhi and Miami are almost the same distance from the equator, but Miami is much more pleasant through the year because it is closer to the sea); how close it is to the desert, and so on.

HOW COME THE EARTH IS CLOSER TO THE SUN DURING SOME PART OF THE YEAR AND FARTHER AWAY AT ANOTHER?

That's because the earth doesn't go around the sun in a perfect circle–its orbit is actually elliptical, or oval. Also, the sun is not bang in the centre of this oval path, it's off to one side. What that means, in a nutshell, is that on one day of the year (usually in early January), the earth is closer to the sun than at any other time, and on a different day (usually in early July), the earth is further away from the sun than at any other time.

The point on the earth's orbit when it is closest to the sun is called the Perihelion (in Latin, 'peri' means near, and 'Helios' is the sun), and the point where it is furthest away is called the Aphelion. Now here's the fun part: at Perihelion, the earth is about 5 million km closer to the sun than it is at Aphelion, but the northern hemisphere is actually freezing then! And at Aphelion, in July, it is sweltering even though the sun is so far away!

Fine, let's forget the northern hemisphere for now, considering it is tilted away from the sun in January and tilted towards the sun in July. What about the southern hemisphere? Sure, the southern hemisphere does have summer when the Perihelion is reached, and winter at Aphelion, but if you look at the temperatures in say, Melbourne, Australia, they are not particularly high in January (the average temperature is about 35 degrees Celsius) or particularly low in July (the average is around 15 degrees Celsius)!

SO THE SAME AMOUNT OF SUNLIGHT REACHES THE EARTH WHETHER WE ARE CLOSER TO OR FURTHER AWAY FROM THE SUN?

Not really. The killer fact is that the intensity of sunlight falling on the earth at Perihelion, when the earth is closest to the sun, is 7 per cent MORE than at Aphelion, when it is furthest. And yet, the average temperature of the entire earth is about 2 degrees HIGHER when it is at Aphelion than when it is at Perihelion! How is that possible?

To understand how that is possible, we have to think about how land and water are divided on the earth. There is far more land in the northern hemisphere, and far more water in the southern hemisphere. Water heats up slowly but it is able to absorb and retain the heat for far longer than land can. That's why, in July, even though the earth is furthest away from the sun AND the southern hemisphere is tilted away from the sun, Melbourne doesn't even come close to freezing over. All the oceans in the southern hemisphere absorb and store the heat from the slanting rays of the sun, keeping Melbourne warm. Well, warm-ish anyway.

At the same time, in the northern hemisphere, which is tilted towards the sun, all the giant land masses are heating up rapidly, collecting the heat from the direct sunlight through the long summer days, and raising the temperatures to almost unbearable levels.

In January, on the other hand, at the Perihelion, the northern hemisphere is tilted away from the sun and receives only slanting sunlight, and that too for a fewer hours each day. The land tries valiantly to gather as much heat as it can in those few hours, but it rapidly loses heat over the long nights, and never quite manages to catch up to decent temperatures, especially in the temperate zone.

And THAT's why we northerners are snuggling into our razais in January, even though the earth is 5 million kilometres closer to the sun then than it is in July.

HOW COME WHEN I LOOK IN A MIRROR, I'M RIGHT SIDE UP, BUT WHEN I LOOK IN A SHINY SPOON, I'M UPSIDE DOWN?

The answer to both questions comes down to the same thing: the reflection of light. The only difference in these two cases is the SHAPE of the surface off which the light is reflecting.

But first, let's understand something far more fundamental—the process of 'seeing'.

HOW DO WE SEE THINGS, ACTUALLY?

You probably know some of this already. To see something, anything, we need two things—our eyes and our brain, and of course, the 'cable' that connects the two, our optic nerve. Basically, when light—whether it's sunlight or artificial light—strikes an object, it bounces off it. The bounced light travels to your eyes and helps you see the object.

Let's say you're looking at a chair. Thousands of rays of light bounce off every tiny point on the chair and enter your eyes through the cornea (the transparent coating that covers your eye) and the pupil (the small black hole in the centre of your eye). These rays then travel through the lens just behind the pupil.

Something cool happens to the rays of light as they pass through the lens—they get *refracted*. We say a ray of light is refracted when it changes direction. Light changes its speed, and therefore its direction, when it passes from one medium to the other. For instance, light rays change direction when they pass from water to air or from air to water.

You can observe the effects of refraction quite clearly when you put a pencil into a clear glass of water. If you look at the spoon from the top, the pencil appears to be bent at the air-water boundary. If you raise the glass and look at it from the side, it looks broken. In both cases, the pencil looks thicker inside the water than outside it. The reason why the pencil looks broken or bent is because the rays of light have slowed down and changed direction when they moved from air to water, which is denser than air. The reason why the pencil looks thicker is because the water and the glass together act as a magnifying glass.

The cool thing is that this happens only when the pencil is slanting, though. Keep the pencil straight up and look into the water, and you will see that it looks absolutely straight inside the water as well, whether you look at it from the top or from the side. It will still look thicker, though.

Where were we? Ah yes, the lens. Now, since the lens is made up of a different material from the air around, the light rays will change direction, or get refracted, when they pass from air into the lens, and get refracted *again* when they pass out of the lens and into the fluid that fills the eyeball behind the lens. The twice-refracted rays of bounced light from the chair 'converge'– or come together–precisely at the retina, the 'screen' at the back of the eyeball, and a sharp image of the chair appears on the retina. Except… the whole refraction thing has ensured that the refracted rays cross over before they hit the retina, so what we get is an upside-down image of the chair!

The retina is no ordinary surface. It has thousands of photoreceptors–sensors which convert the light rays into electrical signals. These electrical signals zip along the optic nerve and straight to the brain. The brain reads the signals, recreates the image, flips it right side up, then sorts through the millions of 'flash cards' in its memory banks, trying to find a match. Until…a-ha! A match is found! The word corresponding to the image is: Chair.

'Chair!' yells the brain. And finally, you have now 'seen' the chair!

Of course, all this frenetic activity–from the light rays striking the chair to your brain coming up with a word for the object–happens in a matter of microseconds. You see the chair without even realizing what you are doing!

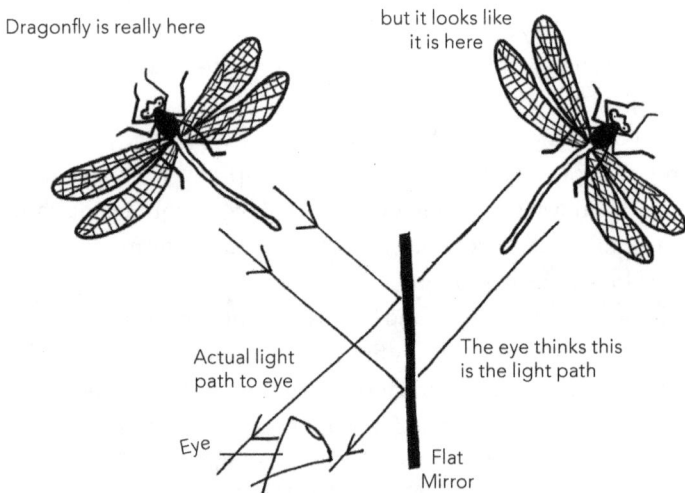

I spy…with my little eye…a dragonfly—why objects behind us seem to be in front of us when we see them through a flat mirror

SO EVERYTHING WE SEE IS REALLY LIGHT BOUNCING OFF THOSE THINGS?

Now, we are used to thinking only of shiny, smooth metallic surfaces–mirrors, for example–as surfaces that are capable of bouncing or reflecting light, and it is true that smoother surfaces reflect light much better. That's why you can see a dark reflection of yourself in glass, still water, and also in smooth, highly polished marble and granite. Oh, and in nicely polished black school shoes as well!

But if it is true that smoothness is necessary for bouncing light rays, and that we can only see things because of the light that bounces off them, how are we able to see objects with rough surfaces as well? Because a rough surface is basically millions of tiny smooth surfaces sitting next to each other, *but with each facing a slightly different direction from its neighbours*! All these tiny smooth surfaces reflect light, but they reflect it in many different directions. This form of reflection is called 'scattering' of light.

So, yes. We see objects because of the light they bounce off or scatter, a part of which falls into our eyes and onto our retinas. That's why we find it so hard to see in the dark!

The reason we can see colour is also because of scattering of light. White objects, in particular, are great scatterers of light. A room with white walls is always much brighter than one with dark walls because it bounces off all colours* and absorbs none. In fact, that's the very reason it looks white to us in the first place.

The reason an object looks red, on the other hand, is because it absorbs all colours EXCEPT red, which it bounces back into the atmosphere. We see an object as black because it absorbs all colours and reflects none. But we can still see black objects because there is no 'perfect' black object, and even black-coloured objects scatter some light.

---

*Light is made up of seven colours—violet, indigo, blue, green, yellow, orange and red. But we don't see these as individual colours, because when these seven colours are combined, our eye sees the result as white light. We only get to see the seven colours when we pass light through a glass prism, or when we see a rainbow, which is created when sunlight is split into its seven colours as it passes through millions of raindrop 'prisms', usually when the sun comes out after a shower.

I STILL DON'T KNOW WHY I GET FLIPPED UPSIDE-DOWN IN A SPOON

We're coming to that. Remember how we spoke of mirrors earlier? The shiny inside of a spoon is also a mirror, and therefore a great reflecting surface. The only difference between a spoon and a flat mirror is just that–the spoon is not flat, but curved. The inside of the spoon is a CONCAVE–or inward-curving–mirror.

Now, concave mirrors treat light very differently from flat mirrors. Flat mirrors don't bend the rays of light falling on them; they just reflect them straight back. Concave mirrors, on the other hand, reflect every ray of light that falls on them at an angle.

To understand why this happens, imagine you are bouncing a basketball on a regular basketball court. The ball bounces straight back up at you. If you bounce it to your left, it bounces away to your left. If you bounce it to your right, it bounces away to your right. The basketball court is your flat mirror and the ball is your ray of light. Because the rays of light hitting a flat surface are reflected straight back, you see an exact, right-side-up image of yourself in a flat mirror.

Bending the rules

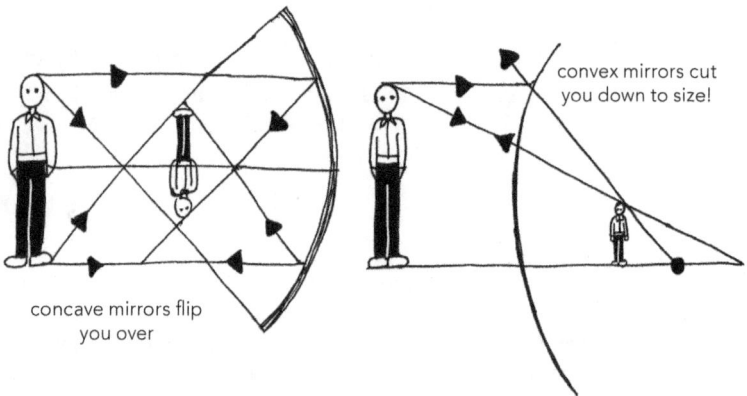

concave mirrors flip
you over

convex mirrors cut
you down to size!

Now imagine you are standing in the centre of a curved bowl-shaped court. If you bounce the ball straight down, it would bounce straight back to you like before. But if you were to bounce it off a wall to your right, it would bounce upwards and off to your left because of the curve of the bowl. If you bounce it at the wall in front of you, it would bounce off and go over your head and behind you. Basically, it would bounce off at an angle and head towards the opposite direction from where you first aimed it. The bowl-shaped court is your concave mirror, and once again, the ball is your ray of light.

Rays of light that hit different points on a concave mirror get bounced off in exactly the same way as the ball, and head towards a direction OPPOSITE to where they came from. And THAT's why you see an inverted image of yourself when you look at a spoon.

HOW COME WATER AT 26 DEG C FEELS UNCOMFORTABLY COLD BUT AIR AT 26 DEG C FEELS LOVELY?

Good question. It is for this very reason that most swimming pools are crowded with swimmers in the summer but start looking deserted the moment the mercury begins to dip. On a pleasant day—when the temperature reads 25 to 26 degrees Celsius—you'd rather play a game of football than strip down to your trunks and go swimming, right? Why does this happen, though? Also, why do we feel cold in the first place?

WHY DO WE FEEL COLD, ANYWAY?

To understand the answer to this question, we should understand what heat is.

Heat is really a form of energy, caused by the movement of molecules in an object. All objects have a certain amount of heat energy. The average amount of heat energy an object has is called its temperature. Bigger substances have more heat energy than smaller ones, simply because they have more molecules. That's why, strange as this may sound, although a lit match has a higher temperature than an ice sculpture, the ice sculpture actually has more heat energy!

Now, why does an object feel cold or hot to us? Being

mammals, we are warm-blooded creatures with a normal body temperature of 37 degrees Celsius. Most things around us are cooler than we are. Now, according to the laws of physics, whenever an object comes in contact with a cooler object, it transfers some of its heat energy to it, until both objects are at the same temperature. When an object comes in contact with a warmer object, it begins to absorb heat from that object.

Our bodies—which are also technically 'objects'—do exactly the same thing. A bar of chocolate out of the fridge begins to melt the longer you hold it because your body is frantically transferring its heat energy to it. At the same time, your body is working hard to maintain its own temperature, because it isn't healthy for your temperature to drop below 37 degrees. The heat transfer (from your body to the chocolate) stops only when the chocolate bar also reaches 37 degrees.

In the same way, we feel cold when we are surrounded by air or water that has a lower temperature than our body temperature, because our body gives away its heat to the air or water around us, and our own body temperature drops. We feel hot when the air around us is of a higher temperature than our own body, because we then begin to absorb heat.

WHAT ARE THE DIFFERENT WAYS IN WHICH HEAT IS 'TRANSFERRED'?

The three main ways in which heat is transferred are—Conduction, Convection and Radiation.

Conduction is when heat is transferred from one body to another by direct contact. When that chocolate melts in your hand, the heat transfer from your body to the chocolate is happening by conduction.

Convection usually happens in fluids.* When you heat a pot

---

*Both liquids and gases are technically fluids because they can be made to move or flow, and because they both will fill a container they are poured into, and take its shape .

of water on a stove, the layer of water at the bottom of the pot, which is closest to the fire, gets heated first (that is, its molecules begin moving faster and faster). This hot layer begins to rise in the pot, and a colder layer rushes in to take its place. Then this layer becomes hot, and begins to rise, and another colder layer comes in to take its place. When the top layer begins to bubble, you know that all the layers have been heated.

The same thing happens in summer. The land gets heated up first, heating up the layer of air closest to it. That layer rises, and a colder layer takes its place, and so on. That's why it gets hotter and hotter as the day progresses—more and more layers of air get heated. As the sun sets and the land begins to cool, the temperature of the air also drops.

Radiation is when waves of heat spread out from a hot object through the air or water around it. It is because of this kind of radiation (combined with convection) that kitchens feel hot when there is a lot of cooking going on, even if you are not actually touching anything hot.

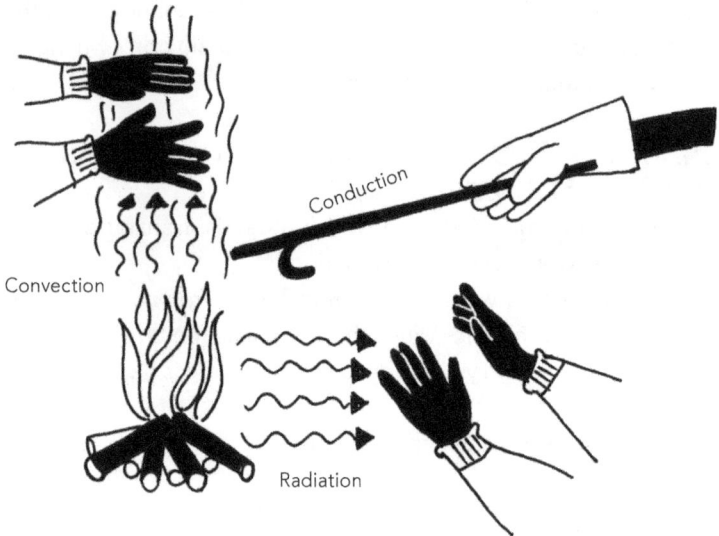

Feeling hot, hot, hot: Three ways in which heat gets transmitted

OKAY, BUT WHY DOES WATER FEEL COLDER THAN AIR?

Ah, yes. The big question. What is important to realize is that, whether it is water at 26 degrees Celsius or air at 26 degrees Celsius, they are both cooler than your body temperature. In both cases, it is your body transferring and losing heat, not the other way around. But water does feel colder than air does, for a bunch of reasons:

- **Water is denser than air.** Since water is a liquid, the molecules in it are closer together than the molecules in air, which is a gas. When you are surrounded by water, your body loses more heat because there are more molecules to heat up.

- **It takes far more energy to heat a certain amount of water than it does to heat the same amount of air.** Why? Because of something called *specific heat* that all substances have, which is a measure of how much energy it takes to heat up a certain amount of that substance. Water has a higher specific heat than air, PLUS there are more molecules of water to heat up!

- **Water is a better conductor of heat than air**. That means it is capable of absorbing the heat that your body is transferring much faster than air is. So heat leaves your body faster when it is in water, and so you feel colder.

- **Heat is required for evaporation**. Notice how you feel less cold when your body is submerged in the pool than when you are standing upright? That's because the water drops sticking to the part of your body exposed to the air begin to evaporate, and for that, they once again use heat from your body! That's why you shiver like mad when you come OUT of the pool and why you should towel off immediately (unless you want to catch a cold!).

So there it is—the answer to the big question. But here's the downside—knowing the answer isn't going to make you feel any less cold the next time you dive into a cold swimming pool. That's life.

HOW IS THE BLOOD IN MY VEINS BLUE WHEN IT IS INSIDE ME, BUT RED WHEN IT COMES OUT?

Sorry, but no, the answer is not, 'Because you are a blueblood, of course!'

NO ONE ever has blue blood. All human blood, which ever way you look at it, is—and always has been—red.

[Never heard of the word 'blueblood'? It's a word used to describe someone of royal birth, a person belonging to an aristocratic or noble family. It probably came into usage because the royals and the aristocrats in medieval times never went out in the sun much, and therefore had prominent blue veins showing through their delicate, pampered, extra pale skins. But their blood still wasn't blue!]

WHAT MAKES BLOOD RED?

What is blood really made of? Well, more than half of it is a straw-yellow liquid called plasma. Plasma is mostly (a whopping 92 per cent of it) nothing but good old water, and it is the 'river' in which other things that make up blood live and float and get around the body. What things? Well, things like:

Red Blood Cells (RBCs) These are the guys that give the blood its red colour. The colour comes from a protein RBCs contain, called haemoglobin, which in turn contains iron. It is haemoglobin that carries fresh oxygen from the lungs to all parts of the body, and it is haemoglobin that carries carbon dioxide back to the lungs from all parts of the body.

White Blood Cells (WBCs) These are our guardian-angel cells, the guys that fight germs and keep us free from disease. They also chomp up cells that are misbehaving or have gotten too old to function.

Platelets These are our bleed-stoppers. When you fall and cut yourself, you automatically stop bleeding after a while, right? Well, it's these guys who make that happen. Whenever you cut yourself, they spring into action, spinning a fine mesh in a twinkling and throwing it across the opening. The RBCs rushing out of the opening get stuck in the mesh, sealing it off, and no more blood is lost!

There are also other things travelling by the plasma 'river'— proteins, fats, glucose and other stuff that is needed by our bodies to function; as well as urea, carbon dioxide and lactic acid—stuff that is not needed by our bodies, which are being taken to places from where they can be thrown out (through urine and poop, for instance).

But to answer our original question at the beginning of this section, what makes our blood red—and it is ALWAYS red—is haemoglobin.

BUT SCIENCE TEXTBOOKS ALWAYS SHOW BLOOD IN OUR VEINS AS BEING BLUE!

Yes, but you are not meant to take it literally. Just because India is coloured pink in the world map in your atlas doesn't mean it is actually pink, does it?

Likewise, it is just a standard across the world to show blood flowing in the arteries (the tubes that carry clean, *fresh* blood from the heart to the rest of the body) as red blood and the blood flowing in the veins (the tubes that carry the 'impure' blood from the rest of the body back to the heart) as blue blood. It doesn't mean that the blood in the veins is actually blue. (What exactly is fresh blood? What does 'impure' blood really mean? Find out in the box on page 124).

> I KNEW IT! HE HAS ALWAYS LIKED FOOTBALL MORE! SEE, HE ISN'T BLEEDING BLUE!

Now, that doesn't mean that the blood in the arteries and the blood in the veins is EXACTLY the same colour. Blood in the arteries is 'clean' blood, which means it has just been pumped out by the heart and is full of just-breathed-in oxygen from the lungs. When haemoglobin mixes with oxygen, it turns a bright crimson, so blood in the arteries is a lovely bright red. Once it has travelled around the body, giving up its oxygen, the same blood returns to the lungs via the veins. But this time, it is laden with carbon dioxide released by various chemical reactions in the body.

Carbon dioxide turns blood a much deeper, darker red, so, yeah, the blood in the veins is a deep maroon, not the bright crimson of artery blood, but it is certainly not blue. You know this for a fact if you've ever had to have a blood test. Blood samples are always drawn from veins because they (the veins) are so close to the surface of the skin, and the blood sample that fills the syringe is red, right?

DOES THE BLOOD IN OUR VEINS LOOK BLUE TO US BECAUSE THE VEINS THEMSELVES ARE BLUE?

Nope. The veins are white, not blue. And the only reason you can see them at all is because they are very close to the surface of the skin, and because their walls are so thin and translucent. (Arteries are much deeper inside the body to protect them from injury, and their walls are much thicker, so you can neither see them nor the blood inside them.)

Why do white veins carrying dark red blood appear blue to us? You see, as we discussed earlier, white light is made up of seven colours. Some substances absorb all seven colours and look black. Some substances don't absorb any colour; instead, they reflect all of them right back. These substances look white to us.

Some substances absorb all colours except one, and reflect just that one back to us. Say you are looking at a sunflower. The sunflower looks yellow because it absorbs all colours EXCEPT yellow, which it bounces back to us. All clear? Let's get to our skin now.

Our translucent skin does not absorb much of any colour of light at all, it just bounces it all back. It is a pigment called melanin in the skin that makes one person's skin look more or less brown than another's. This is why the skin and hair of someone who has very little melanin—think of a blond-haired, blue-eyed German or American—looks pale and light-coloured, almost white.

Unlike skin, blood absorbs all colours of light. But it is not so good at absorbing red, so it bounces it back at us (which is why blood looks red). A little of this red colour is reflected back *through our skin* by the fresh blood from the heart flowing just under it in tiny tubes called capillaries. This is especially noticeable when the heart is pumping hard and the blood supply to your skin increases. That's why you get rosy-cheeked after a round of exercise, flush when you're angry, and blush bright red when you're embarrassed.

Veins are located a little deeper inside the skin, about 0.5 mm deep. The blood in the veins is ready to absorb all the colours of the light falling on your skin, but only some colours can penetrate that far through skin tissue. Blue light is particularly bad at passing through, so it just gets reflected back at us.

And THAT's why our veins look blue to us—because we are looking at them *through our skin*. If we were able to look at our arteries through our skin, they would look blue too! Not because of the colour of blood in them, but because of a trick of the light.

BLOODLINE: HOW BLOOD FLOWS THROUGH OUR BODIES

SEVERAL TIMES EVERY MINUTE, EVERY MINUTE OF YOUR LIFE, YOUR LITTLE FIST-SIZED HEART MAKES SURE FRESH, PURE, OXYGEN-RICH BLOOD REACHES EVERY CELL OF YOUR BODY. BUT HOW DOES FRESH BLOOD REACH THE HEART IN THE FIRST PLACE? AND HOW DOES IT THEN REACH EVERY LITTLE CELL OF YOUR BODY? LET'S FIND OUT.

BASICALLY, THERE ARE THREE MAIN PLAYERS INVOLVED IN THIS WHOLE PROCESS OF TAKING FRESH BLOOD AROUND THE BODY—THE HEART, THE LUNGS, AND THE BLOOD VESSELS, WHICH ARE BASICALLY THE TUBES THROUGH WHICH BLOOD FLOWS. THE HEART IS THE PUMP, THE LUNGS ARE THE SWAP-THE-BAD-STUFF-WITH-THE-GOOD-STUFF SYSTEM AND THE BLOOD VESSELS ARE THE COURIERS.

THE HEART HAS FOUR CHAMBERS OR SECTIONS, TWO ON THE RIGHT SIDE AND TWO ON THE LEFT. IMPURE BLOOD—BLOOD WITH VERY LITTLE OXYGEN IN IT—FROM ALL OVER THE BODY IS COLLECTED AND BROUGHT TO THE TOP RIGHT

CHAMBER OF THE HEART BY BLOOD VESSELS CALLED VEINS. FROM HERE, THEY PASS TO THE BOTTOM RIGHT CHAMBER, AND THEN TO THE LUNGS. IN THE LUNGS, THE BLOOD GIVES UP THE CARBON DIOXIDE IT IS CARRYING FOR THE LUNGS TO GET RID OF. AT THE SAME TIME, IT LOADS UP WITH FRESH OXYGEN THAT THE LUNGS HAVE JUST BREATHED IN. THIS 'CLEAN' BLOOD GOES BACK TO THE HEART, AND EMPTIES INTO THE TOP LEFT CHAMBER. FROM HERE, IT TRAVELS TO THE BOTTOM LEFT CHAMBER, AND FROM THERE INTO BLOOD VESSELS CALLED ARTERIES. IT IS ARTERIES THAT TAKE FRESH BLOOD ALL OVER THE BODY.

ARTERIES AND VEINS ARE NOT THE ONLY KINDS OF BLOOD VESSELS THERE ARE, THEY ARE JUST THE MAJOR ONES. BIG FAT ARTERIES LEADING OUT OF THE HEART BRANCH OFF INTO SMALL ARTERIES WHICH FURTHER BRANCH INTO ARTERIOLES, WHICH TAKE THE FRESH BLOOD TO VARIOUS 'DEPARTMENTS'–SKIN, MUSCLE, BONES, ETC. THESE ARTERIOLES THEN BRANCH INTO THE SMALLEST OF ALL BLOOD VESSELS, THE MICROSCOPIC CAPILLARIES, WHICH ACTUALLY DROP OFF NUTRIENTS INTO INDIVIDUAL CELLS AND PULL OUT THE WASTES FROM THEM. ON THE WAY BACK, CAPILLARIES JOIN TO FORM VENULES, WHICH JOIN TO FORM THE BIGGER VEINS, WHICH CARRY WASTE MATTER FROM ALL THE BODY'S CELLS BACK TO THE TOP RIGHT CHAMBER OF THE HEART, WHERE THE PROCESS BEGINS ALL OVER AGAIN.

HOW COME NO ONE FINDS THE WEIGHT THEY LOSE?

Look around you. Everyone around us seems to be trying to lose weight. A few of them actually do lose weight and then turn into the biggest bores in the world as they go on and on about the number of kilos they have 'dropped'. Dropped, huh? Where? How come we never get to see those hundreds of kilos dropped by hundreds of people? Either the municipality is doing a fabulous job cleaning up after these weight-droppers, OR—and this is far more likely—they are all lying.

Actually, neither of these is the truth. Nor is there witchcraft or wizardry involved. So where does all the lost weight go, then?

WHY ARE PEOPLE FAT IN THE FIRST PLACE?

A good supporting question to that is—what happens to the food we eat? Any food we eat—whether it is good, nutritious food or complete junk—has at least one (and usually more than one) of the following seven basic components that our body needs to function well: carbohydrates, proteins, fats, vitamins, minerals, fibre and water.

Of course, none of the food we eat comes neatly divided into these seven categories—if it did, life would be very boring indeed. Instead, food looks like apples and pizza and samosas and double chocolate chip cookies—none of which is of any use to the body in its original form. The wonder of our digestive systems is that they

126

can take all the random food we eat and turn it into something our bodies can actually use.

Now, our bodies require energy to digest our food, which in turn comes from the food itself. The energy contained in the food we eat is measured in calories. When our bodies have finished breaking down our food, the blood takes away the carbohydrates, proteins, fats and everything else to where they are needed. The calories left over after digestion are used for other jobs. If there are still some calories left over, the body converts them into fat and stores the fat in 'fat cells'.

Why is fat stored, and not simply thrown out of the body? Because of lessons the body has learnt through evolution. Thousands of years ago, when man was a hunter-gatherer, he did not know when or what he would eat next or where that food would come from. So the body learnt to store extra energy from food as fat so that if the next meal was too long coming, it could simply reconvert the stored fat back into energy to keep the body running.

These days, of course, most of us know when and where our next meal is coming from (from the neighbourhood store, in a potato chip packet, whenever we feel like it). But the body

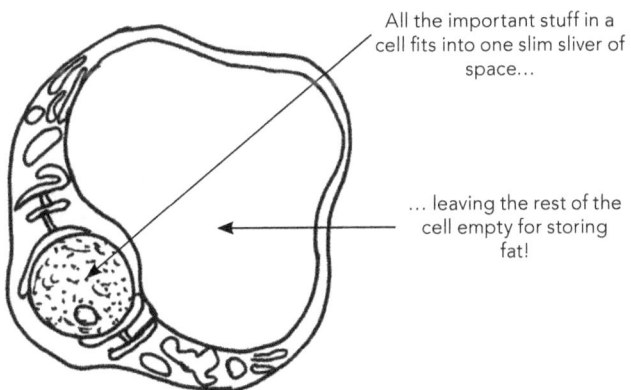

All the important stuff in a cell fits into one slim sliver of space…

… leaving the rest of the cell empty for storing fat!

The fat truth: What a 'fat cell' really looks like

continues to store extra calories as fat. Because you eat fairly regular meals, however, the extra calories never get a chance to get used. Instead, more extra calories are released, which are in turn converted into fat. Your fat cells get bigger and bigger, and so does your waist size!

In the beginning, you have the same number of fat cells as anyone else. Even stevens.

As you load up on junk food in front of the TV, your original fat cells get full up with fat. New fat cells are created, and you put on weight. Uh-oh.

You stop eating the junk, start exercising, and lose the excess weight. Hurray!

After a while, you get back to your old ways, and regain weight. But you put on more weight than other people eating the same food, because all those EXTRA fat cells from the last time are still around! Bummer.

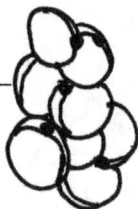

Once you buy a fat cell, it's yours for life

The trick, of course, is to only eat as many calories as your body needs, or, if you eat more, to burn the extra calories by exercising regularly.

But, you wail, there are so many people who eat whatever junk they like and never put on an inch while I put on weight just by standing next to a doughnut! Well, it might LOOK that way, but chances are those people are just doing some small things differently from you. For one thing, they may be more active than you. That may not necessarily mean that they play a sport regularly, but just that they stand around a lot, or pace up and down when they are talking to someone, or take the stairs two at a time, or just are extremely fidgety and restless, all of which is activity that burns calories.

Activity also builds muscle, and you need to burn a lot more calories to maintain muscle than you need to burn to maintain fat. A third reason may be that while that 'lucky' friend of yours seems to eat only junk when he is with you, he probably eats quite healthy at home because his mom insists on it.

HOW DO PEOPLE 'LOSE' WEIGHT?

Now that you know how you 'put on' weight, it is fairly obvious how you can lose weight. Basically, *you have to burn more calories than you take in*. If the food you eat does not create enough energy for your body's needs, your body will revert to 'caveman mode' and begin pulling out the extra calories stored in your fat cells and burning them to create the extra fuel it needs. What happens to the fat cells? They shrink, and so does your waistline!

Some people lose weight by eating less, some through exercising, and some, by both. Not much energy is required to slouch in front of a television, unfortunately, but plenty is required for a game of football or tennis. Where will that energy come from if it doesn't come from overeating? From your body's stored fat, of course!

But then, isn't it a good idea to stop eating almost completely? Wouldn't weight loss be much faster if you ate very little, or ate only once a day? Unfortunately, that's not how your body works. When you eat very little, your body imagines a famine is coming, goes into panic mode, and starts *hoarding* the fat it has stored. Instead of breaking fat down for energy, it begins breaking down the protein stored in your muscles to stay alive. Since muscle cells are mostly made up of water, a lot of water leaves your body when they are broken down, and your weighing scales may show that you have lost weight. But you are actually not losing your fat, you are losing your *protein*. And this could actually make you fatter instead of thinner!

Because, you see, muscles are great calorie-burners. The more muscle you have, the more efficiently your body burns calories. Lose muscle, and the few calories you do take in get burnt much more slowly, and instead get stored as more fat! So, give up the idea of starting a crazy diet to lose weight. The ONLY way is to eat right and exercise.

BUT WHERE DOES THE LOST WEIGHT GO?

Nowhere! The laws of physics state that matter can neither be created nor destroyed; it just gets converted from one form to another. In this case, when you lose weight, what is really happening is that your fat cells are popping the fat they had been storing back into your body, where it is converted into energy that your body can use.

BUT the fat cells themselves don't go away when you lose weight. So if you begin to chow down more than your body needs a couple of months later, well, the fat cells are going to get fat and happy all over again. And then you WILL find the weight you lost—inside yourself! Hyuk, hyuk.

WHY ARE CHIMPS-OUR CLOSEST COUSINS-SO HAIRY WHEN WE AREN'T?

Why, really? Why did evolution pick *us*–and not the chimps, the gorillas, the orang-utans or the gibbons–to be the 'Naked Apes'?

Okay. Big confession coming up right at the outset–no one is quite sure. But there are a lot of interesting theories floating around and a lot of research is being done in this area, so don't stop reading! The other, related question is: How come we have so much hair on our heads (well, some of us, anyway) and so little elsewhere on our bodies?

HOW CLOSELY ARE WE RELATED TO THE OTHER APES, REALLY?

Very, very closely, as a matter of fact. To understand just how closely, we must look at Darwin's theory of evolution. Essentially, evolutionary scientists and anthropologists believe that ALL living things–bacteria, plants, cockroaches, spiders, fish, birds, snakes, the T-Rex, pigs, monkeys, chimps, humans–had a single common 'universal' ancestor 3.5 billion years ago. Yeah, tough to believe, especially since all these life-forms are so different from one another, but true.

Let's think of this unnamed universal ancestor as the trunk of a gigantic family tree of living organisms. Some 1.6 billion years ago, the trunk branched off into two and began to grow apart—one branch had bacteria, the other had organisms with cells that were different from the bacteria cells in one important way. The new kind of cell had something extra in it—a little bag called a nucleus, packed full of genetic material ('genetic material' is basically the set of instructions that helps a cell make another cell exactly like itself).

This new cell, called a *eukaryotic cell* because it had a nucleus, became the ancestor of every living thing that came after, or more simply, everything except bacteria. The eukaryotic branch of the family tree took off, branching over and over again into different families of creatures, from fungi, insects and molluscs to amphibians, reptiles, birds... Finally, some 70 million years ago, a new branch sprouted from the family tree. The hairy mammals—warm-blooded animals like us who give birth to young ones, suckle them, and yes, have HAIR, unlike ALL the other living things that came before—had arrived.

Over 55 million years later, a new twig burst out of the mammal branch and began reaching for the stars. Scientists call this twig Hominidae. From this twig came all the great apes. Over the next 13 million years, the Hominidae twig branched off first into the orang-utans, a little later into the gorillas, and even later, just about 5 million years ago, into humans on one side, and chimpanzee-like creatures on the other. Only 2 million years ago, the chimp-like branch split again, giving us two distinct apes—chimpanzees and bonobos.

What does this mean, really? Think about your own family. You are more like your sibling than your cousin because you and your sibling have a more recent common ancestor (your parents) than you and your cousin (where your grandparents are your most recent common ancestor). Similarly, since chimpanzees, bonobos and humans have a more recent common ancestor than any other pair of living species, they share more similarities with each other than with *any* other living creature!

In fact, recent studies have shown that orang-utan DNA and human DNA are 96.9 per cent alike, gorilla and human DNA are 98.4 per cent alike, and chimp or bonobo DNA and human DNA are 98.8 per cent alike! But since even a tiny 1.2 per cent difference in DNA could mean about 35 *million* differences in body structure, appearance, behaviour and function, it isn't surprising that you can usually tell when you're looking at a human and when you are looking at a chimp.

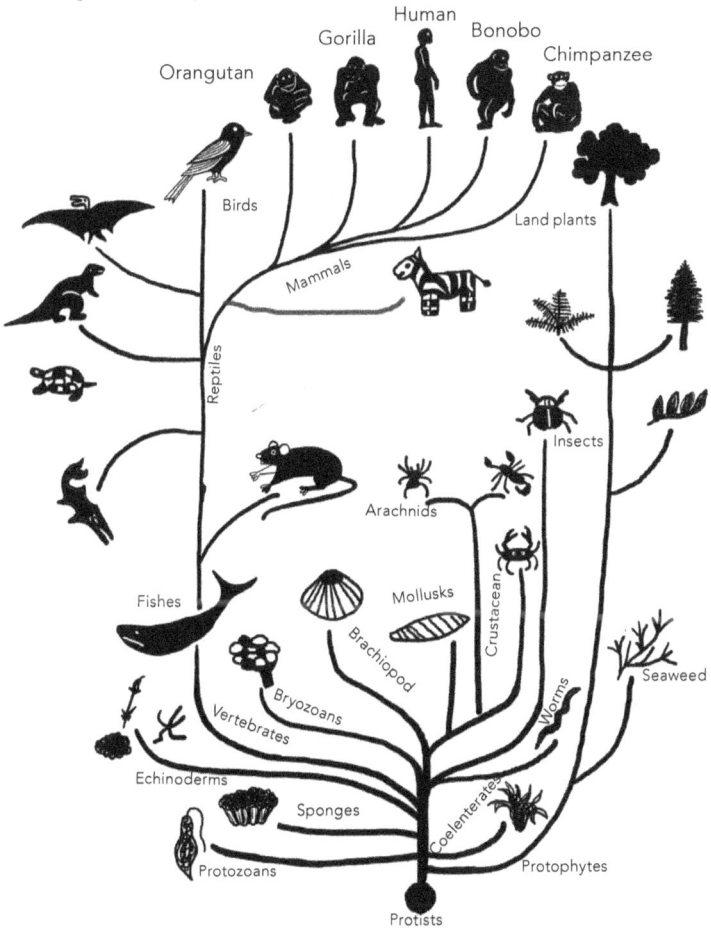

It took 3.6 billion years of evolution to create the Naked Apes—us!

Particularly because chimps are so much hairier than humans. (Even though they are far less hairy than other apes).

HOW AND WHY DID HUMANS LOSE THEIR HAIR?

The Cool-Dude Theory: This is probably the most popular one of them all, and it contends that we lost our hair to keep cool. Like all other monkeys and apes, we humans were also tree-dwelling, until we decided to come down. Jungles were cooler than the hot savannah into which we descended, and our thick fur became a real pain to deal with, because it made us even hotter. The less hairy among our ancestors survived better in the hot climate, and over thousands of generations of less hairy survivors, we became slowly hairless. OR. As our brains got bigger than those of the other apes, more heat was produced in our bodies which needed to be got rid of. One way was to develop sweat glands, which very few other living creatures have. Another was to lose the fur.

- **Big gaping holes in the theory**: Well firstly, being hairless and cool is all very well during the day, but what about all the shivering that would happen at night, when a fur cover would have been very welcome? Secondly, there are *many* hairy monkeys living in savannas today, and they seem to manage just fine. Plus, chimps, who also have less hair than gorillas and other apes, still live in cool jungles.

The Something-Fishy Theory: Some 8 million years ago, our ape-like ancestors were semi-aquatic, and spent a lot of time foraging for food in water. Now, everyone knows that fur doesn't really keep you warm in water. But what does keep you warm is blubber, the layer of fat other aquatic mammals have under their skins. So we lost our fur, and started storing fat under our skins. That's why we have higher body fat levels than chimps and other non-aquatic mammals, and that's why we tend to put on weight easily.

- **Big gaping holes in the theory**: Firstly, there's no fossil evidence to show that our ape-like ancestors ever swam around looking for food. And secondly, although we don't like to hear it, we put on weight because we eat the wrong foods and lounge around in front of the television. So stop blaming evolution and go for a walk already!

The Don't-Let-Sleeping-Lice-Lie Theory: Fur is Disneyland for all kinds of parasites. Lice, ticks, mites, small biting flies, and what-have-you gather there in hordes to play and feast on your blood, alternately giving you horrible diseases and making you itch madly. Once humans learnt how to build fires, make shelters for themselves, and use animal skins to cover their bodies—all of which would help them to keep warm even without fur—they simply shed their pesky fur forever.

- **Big gaping holes in the theory**: Well, if humans were so smart, why did they keep the hair on their heads then? Head lice are such a problem, even today! Some argue that they probably kept it to protect their heads from the sun and to keep the heads warm in the cold, and also because, like a bird's decorative plumage, it was attractive to the opposite sex!

Well, anyway, the jury is still out on this one. If you have any theories of your own, just bung them in the pot too. They have as much possibility of being right as any of the others—because science does not really have the answer to this one yet.

BUT WHY DOESN'T SCIENCE HAVE ALL THE ANSWERS?

That's a great question to ask at the end of a book like this. Especially because it is the truth—science truly does not have all the answers. Sure, science is patient and perseverant and accurate and creative and very, very good at finding out facts. It can tell us exactly how fast light travels and why we look like our parents. It can explain why the moon stays in orbit around the earth and how a chameleon changes colour. It can give us the information we need to build a car and help us, step by fascinating step, to understand the wonders of nature.

But science cannot explain why we find kittens adorable or why ice is slippery. It can't tell us what makes people fall in love or why listening to a piece of music can make us sad. It has no accurate answers to the questions, 'How many animal species are there in the world?' or 'Why do we laugh?' It cannot tell us how to live our lives, how often to wash our socks, or how to be good or kind. And it definitely, definitely, cannot tell us if there is a God.

But what is science, really? Just the collective knowledge of the human race—OUR race. And because *humans* don't have all the answers yet, neither does science. The good news, though, is that one of the unique qualities that we humans have is our boundless curiosity. Another is our never-ending dissatisfaction with the way things are. Which may sound like a negative thing, but isn't, really, because it is this discontent that keeps us pushing and pushing for ways to improve the way things are, which is really the starting point for new discoveries.

So maybe, one day, science will have all the answers. Because, you see, science *never stops trying*. As long as there are phenomena to be observed and machines to be invented and new worlds to be discovered and puzzles to be cracked, science will keep going, slowly but steadily peeling off the layers of mystery that shroud our universe. As it uncovers more and more wonders, it will find ways of turning all the new stuff it has discovered to its, and our, advantage.

Also, maybe it is a good thing science doesn't have all the answers. Because, if it did, there would be nothing left for you to discover when you grow up, would there? And THAT would be a real shame.

So get out there, and observe, record, experiment, analyse, hypothesize, theorize, fail, try again, fail again, try again, DISCOVER! The universe is your oyster—what are you waiting for?